Mattison
May you all know
of goodness
— Rabbi & Gilde

A TIME TO HEAL

THE LUBAVITCHER REBBE'S RESPONSE
TO LOSS AND TRAGEDY

D1606401

MENDEL KALMENSON

Chabad.ORG
718-735-2000
editor@chabad.org

Excerpts from Sifrei Hasichot
and letters by the Lubavitcher Rebbe of righteous memory
are used with permission from Kehot Publication Society.

Published by
EZRA PRESS
770 Eastern Parkway, Brooklyn, New York 11213
718-774-4000 / Fax 718-774-2718
editor@kehot.com

Order Department:
291 Kingston Avenue, Brooklyn, New York 11213
718-778-0226 / Fax 718-778-4148
www.kehot.com

EZRA PRESS is an imprint of Kehot Publication Society.
The Ezra logo is a trademark of Kehot Publication Society.

EZRA
PRESS

ISBN: 978-0-8266-9001-2

Printed in The United States of America

To every thing there is a season,

And a time to every purpose under the heaven:

A time to be born, and a time to die;

A time to plant, and a time to pluck up that which is planted;

A time to kill, and A Time to Heal;

A time to break down, and a time to build up;

A time to weep, and a time to laugh;

A time to mourn, and a time to dance;

A time to cast away stones, and a time to gather stones together;

A time to embrace, and a time to refrain from embracing;

A time to get, and a time to lose;

A time to keep, and a time to cast away;

A time to rend, and a time to sew;

A time to keep silence, and a time to speak;

A time to love, and a time to hate;

A time of war, and a time of peace.

ECCLESIASTES, 3:1-8

This book is dedicated to Dr. Mark Glaser
who embodies the teaching of our Sages:

"He who saves a life
is considered to have saved the entire world."

SACHA AND TANYA GAYDAMAK

TABLE OF CONTENTS

I. DEALING WITH PERSONAL TRAGEDY

The profound loneliness of grief can be eased with the
knowledge that one's loss is shared by others.

Mitigating the feeling of loss through the understanding that the soul lives on.

A connection still exists with the departed soul, even
if it is more spiritual in nature.

The mourning periods outlined by the Torah provide
a framework for grieving.

The belief that there is a constant Higher force in our

lives Who is deeply concerned with our well-being enables us to overcome our darkest moments.

II. HELPING OTHERS COPE WITH LOSS

III. RESPONSES TO SOCIETAL AND GLOBAL TRAGEDIES

PREFACE

There is much to be said about content in the Internet age. Online, it is accessible instantly to all, superseding the traditional barriers of mobility, affiliation and more. Yet, after twenty years of creating and publishing Jewish content online, and with tens of millions of annual visitors to our website and other digital channels, we are delighted to present you with this printed volume.

The printed word fills our physical space with wisdom in the form of tangible ink and paper. Indeed, one of the mitzvah campaigns the Rebbe, of righteous memory, spearheaded worldwide was *Bayit Malei Seforim* ("house full of Jewish books"), encouraging everyone to acquire printed Torah literature in order to create a holy atmosphere in the home.

We are very grateful for our partnership with Ezra Press, an imprint of the Kehot Publication Society. The official publishing house of the Chabad-Lubavitch movement, Kehot has for more than seventy years brought Chasidic, Halachic and Kabbalistic teachings to millions. We look forward to serving the reading public together for many years to come.

Chabad.org

20 Menachem Av, 5775
Brooklyn, NY

NOTE ON TRANSLATION:

Many of the quotations from the Rebbe's teachings were not originally delivered in English, and have been adapted for this work.

INTRODUCTION

Have you ever been so overcome by emotion that you were at a loss for words? Have you ever felt that you not only lacked the appropriate words but were even confused about how to think and feel in response to a particular event?

Many of us experience this type of disorientation when we are faced with tragic events—whether they occur in our lives, in the lives of those around us, or even on a global scale. In addition to the feelings of grief and loss that we are experiencing, we may also feel confused about how to cope with these feelings. How should we respond to what has happened? How do we deal with the sense of loss and the feelings of loneliness that come with it? This confusion can make our internal experience overwhelming and sometimes debilitating.

While the belief in the loving guidance of a Higher Power and in the meaningfulness of our existence offers great comfort in times of tragedy and loss, such belief brings its own set of challenges and questions at such times: Is it permitted to question G-d or complain about His ways? What place is there for personal grief if we believe that G-d is just and that the soul of our loved one lives on?

If, as the Sages of Israel teach, the ultimate truth is that "no evil descends from Above,"[1] where can we turn to find meaning in disaster? And, supposing we do come to find meaning in our suffering, or in some way come to terms with catastrophe, aren't we then condoning the existence of suffering in the world?

These issues have been discussed by Jewish scholars throughout history, and their conclusions reflect a variety of perspectives. Some espouse the need to maintain a solid faith in the face of suffering in spite of human frailty, while others make space for people to express a range of human emotions at the expense of unquestioning faith.

Our generation was blessed with a unique Jewish leader, the Lubavitcher Rebbe, Rabbi Menachem M. Schneerson, of righteous memory, who embodied both tremendous faith in G-d and a deep love for humanity. Over the course of his four decades of leadership, the Rebbe responded to many tragic events that took place in the Jewish community. What follows is a collection of his reactions to those events and the guidance he offered, highlighting the manner in which he incorporated both staunch devotion to G-d and deep compassion for mankind in his responses.

In the Rebbe's correspondence with the bereaved, there is both an insistence that all events are part of a divine plan and that everything happens for the best as well as a very real acceptance of human suffering and its expression. In the Rebbe's worldview, expressions of faith and expressions of human vulnerabilities are not contradictory. Gratitude for the life that was can find expression alongside grief, and unwavering faith can coexist even with a challenge to G-d's ways.

It is my sincere hope that those who have suffered loss, as well as those looking for a way to approach others' losses, are able to find guidance and solace somewhere in the warm words that follow.

Mendel Kalmenson

PART I

DEALING WITH PERSONAL TRAGEDY

CHAPTER 1

SHARED LOSS

One of the very difficult aspects of bereavement is the feeling that we are utterly alone in our misery—that no other human being can possibly share in the depth of our loss.

This feeling only intensifies when the rest of the world moves on, having barely paused to take notice of the devastating hole that death has punched in our universe. This experience of profound loneliness can be eased somewhat by a sense of solidarity with others, a sense that our loss, while deeply personal, is also shared by the wider community.

In October of 1967, a few months after the Six-Day War, a terrible tragedy struck the home of Ariel Sharon, the famous Israeli general and future prime minister of Israel.

Sharon's eleven-year-old son Gur was playing outdoors with a friend. The two children were fooling around with an old shotgun, which belonged to the general, when the other boy pointed the gun at Gur's head and mistakenly pulled the trigger.

When he heard the shot, Sharon rushed outside, where he found his son Gur lying unconscious in a pool of blood. Sharon knew the wound was fatal, yet, still hoping, he took him in his arms and flagged down a passing car to take him to the nearest hospital. A short while later, Gur was gone, having died in his father's arms.

A Chabad rabbi came to visit Sharon during the week of mourning. The room was full of generals and politicians. A devastated Ariel Sharon pulled the rabbi aside and peppered him with questions, imploring, "You are religious; tell me, how could this happen?" The rabbi could only suggest that he ask the Lubavitcher Rebbe for answers.

"But why should I write to him? He doesn't know me."

"The Rebbe feels the pain of every Jew," was the reply.

After leaving Sharon's home, the rabbi made contact with the Rebbe and informed him about Sharon's anguished questions. The Rebbe immediately reached out to Sharon with a letter, which included the following message:

I was deeply grieved to read in the newspaper about the tragic loss of your tender, young son, may he rest in peace....

At first glance, it would appear that we are distant from one another, not only geographically, but also—or even more so—in terms of being unfamiliar, indeed, unaware of each other, until the Six-Day War (as it's come to be known), when you became famous and celebrated as a commander and defender of our Holy Land and its inhabitants.... But on the basis of a fundamental, deeply rooted, age-old Jewish principle, namely, that all Jews are kindred, the fame you received served to reveal something that existed even before—that is, the interconnectedness of all Jews, including between a Jew who lives in the Holy Land and a Jew who lives in the Diaspora. It is this interconnectedness that spurred me to write these words to you and your family....

An element of solace—indeed, more than just an element—even in so great a tragedy is expressed in the traditional text [of the words spoken to a mourner], hallowed by scores of generations of Torah and tradition among our people: "May the Omnipresent comfort you among the mourners of Zion and Jerusalem."

On the face of it, the connection [between the individual mourner and the mourners of the destruction of Jerusalem and the Holy Temple] appears to be quite puzzling. In truth, however, the main consolation embodied by this phrase is in its inner content: namely, that just as the grief over Zion and Jerusalem is common to all the sons and daughters of Israel wherever they may be (although it is more palpable to those who dwell in Jerusalem and actually see the Western Wall and the ruins of our Holy Temple than to those who are far away from it; nonetheless, even those who are far experience great pain and grief over the destruction), so too is the grief of a single individual Jew or Jewish family shared by the entire nation. This itself is a source of consolation. For as our Sages expressed themselves,[2] all the people of Israel constitute one complete entity....[3]

The Rebbe was reminding Sharon of an essential truth: we are not alone. The Jewish nation is a single unit. Our private joys are the joys of our people; our losses are the losses of our nation.

CHAPTER 2

ETERNITY OF THE SOUL

Along with the experience of loneliness, one of the most acutely painful aspects of bereavement is the feeling of loss. A person whom we knew and loved—possibly for an entire lifetime—is now gone.

After experiencing the death of a loved one, it can be difficult to move forward while harboring this continual sense of loss. The feeling of emptiness can be overwhelming and paralyzing.

For the believer, the ultimate source of comfort is the knowledge that the void and absence that death leaves behind is only temporary. A foundational principle of the Jewish faith is the belief in *techiyat ha-meitim* ("resurrection of the dead"), which will occur in the messianic era, as prophesied by the prophets of Israel.[4] Still, in the interim, a dear and beloved person has been removed from our lives. How is one to cope with this devastating reality on a day-to-day basis?

In his communications with people who were

grieving, the Rebbe emphasized that from a spiritual perspective, the loss of a loved one is not the complete loss we oftentimes consider it to be.

In the previous chapter, we quoted the Rebbe's letter to Ariel Sharon, in which the Rebbe cites the traditional words of consolation spoken to a mourner, "May the Omnipresent comfort you among the mourners of Zion and Jerusalem," and sees in these words a message on how the burden of grief is shared by the entire community. In that same letter, the Rebbe touches on two additional messages of consolation that can be derived from the connection between the individual mourner's grief and that of the mourners of Zion and Jerusalem:

> Just as we have complete confidence that God will certainly rebuild the ruins of Zion and Jerusalem, gather the dispersed of Israel from all corners of the world through the righteous Moshiach, and bring them joyfully to witness the rejoicing of Zion and Jerusalem, so do we trust that regarding the loss of the individual mourner, God will fulfill his promise, "Awake and rejoice, you who repose in the dust,"[5] and we will experience true joy when all are reunited with the future resurrection of the dead.

There is yet a third point: Just as in regard to Zion and Jerusalem, the Romans, and before them, the

Babylonians, were given dominion only over the wood and stone, silver and gold of the physical Holy Temple but not over its inner, spiritual essence, felt within the heart of each and every Jew—for the nations have no dominion over this, and it stands eternally—so too, regarding the mourning of the individual: Death has dominion only regarding the physical body and the physical aspects of the deceased person. The soul, however, is eternal; it has simply ascended to the World of Truth....[3]

In a letter written by the Rebbe in 1978 to a family in Milan who had experienced a death in the family, the Rebbe writes:

> The only thing that an illness or a fatal accident can do is cause a weakening or termination of the bond that holds the body and soul together, whereupon the soul departs from its temporary abode in this world and returns to its original world of pure spirit in the eternal world.[6]

On April 13, 1973, during a public address he gave on the occasion of his seventy-first birthday, the Rebbe spoke movingly about those who had perished in the Holocaust.

> "A sword or gun, fire or flood can affect only the physical body or the soul's connection to

the body, but never the soul itself. If you ask a rational individual, "What is the person's essence, his body or soul? With whom are you truly connected? Who is precious to you? Whom do you defend, and whose pain alarms you?"—he will acknowledge that it is the soul.

What does this tell us? The beloved soul with whom one had a connection, who was sent to Auschwitz and there gave his life for being a Jew—the body may have taken, but the soul remains.

"The soul remains the day after Auschwitz, a year after Auschwitz, and a generation after Auschwitz… the soul remains whole into eternity."[7]

In 1960, a group of college students came to see the Rebbe. One of the topics they discussed was the Jewish understanding of death.

The Rebbe explained: "The term used to describe death in Judaism is *histalkut*, which does not mean death in the sense of coming to an end, but rather an elevation from one level to another. When one completes his or her mission in life, the departed person is elevated to a higher plane.

"So death is not a cessation of life, but rather describes the process whereby one's spiritual life takes on a new dimension. This notion is consistent with the scientific principle of conservation of matter, which states that nothing physical can be annihilated. This table or a piece of iron can be cut up, burned, etc., but in no instance can the matter of the table or the iron be destroyed. It only takes on a different form.

"Likewise, on the spiritual level, our spiritual being—the soul—can never be destroyed. It only changes its form or is elevated to a different plane.

"Accordingly," the Rebbe concluded, "the term 'afterlife' is actually inappropriate, for what we experience after death is a continuation of life. Until 120 (the human lifespan mentioned in the Torah), life is experienced on one level, and from 121, 122, and 123 onward, it is carried on at another level, and we continue to ascend higher and higher in the realm of the spirit."[8]

On the evening of December 31st, 1952, Rabbi Yaakov Yisrael Zuber, dean of the Lubavitcher yeshiva in Boston and rabbi at Congregation Beth Hamidrash Hagodol in Roxbury, Massachusetts, was attacked by muggers who beat him so severely that he died. This man had survived Stalinist Russia with his religious integrity intact, only to be murdered in the safe haven of the United States. The Rebbe sent representatives from Brooklyn to the funeral and reached out to the family. A few months later Chana Zuber (today Chana Sharfstein), the daughter of Rabbi Zuber, came with her mother to New York for a *yechidut* (private audience) with the Rebbe. She established a warm rapport with the Rebbe and remained in contact with him over the years.

Tragically, less than five years after the death of Chana's father, her mother, Rebbetzin Zlata Zuber, suffered a fatal stroke and passed away the following day. Utterly devastated, Chana requested a *yechidut*, at which she told the Rebbe of the great emotional pain she was still experiencing and asked for guidance on how to deal with her grief. The Rebbe responded by revisiting a few points he had made to her in the condolence letter he sent her upon her mother's passing: "All believers in G-d believe also in the survival of the soul. Actually, this principle has even been discovered in the physical world, where science now holds, as an absolute truth, that nothing in the world can be physically destroyed. How much more so in the spiritual world, especially in the case of the soul, which in no way can be affected by the death and disintegration of the physical body...."[9]

The Rebbe acknowledged the pain that people experience when someone dear to them passes on, the terrible void that is felt because one can no longer touch, hug, or converse with the deceased. But if the most important attachment we have with the people we love is to the quality of their soul, "including such spiritual things as character, kindness, goodness, all of which are attributes of the soul and not of the body," the loss and devastation will be less acute. We can summarize the Rebbe's view thus: When you love a person, you love what the person is, you love the person's character, his personality. And those are things that cannot be destroyed.

When my uncle, Rabbi Yitzchak Vorst, lost his two-year-old son to a fatal car accident, he drew enormous comfort from the Rebbe's teachings. Rabbi Vorst subsequently wrote a book, *Why? Reflections on the Loss of a Loved One*, in which he communicates the Rebbe's message of solace and comfort to others who, like him, have suffered bereavement.

To illustrate this concept, Rabbi Vorst provides his own analogy of a television broadcast: a transmitting station broadcasts images and sounds in the form of energy waves, which are received by a physical device that displays them. Imagine that something goes wrong with the device itself, so that its screen and speakers no longer display the ideas, feelings, and actions encoded within the energy waves. But the transmitting station, and the energy waves incorporating the media, exist no less than before; it is only that the physical receiving device is no longer translating them into physically visible and audible phenomena. By way of analogy, says Rabbi Vorst, we can envision the soul itself as the transmitting station (i.e., the source of the person's personality, character, thoughts, emotions, actions, etc.) and the body as the receiving device. The death of the body does not in any way affect the integrity of the soul, nor does it halt the soul's self-expression (analogous to the energy waves that are emanating through space); it is only that we have been deprived of the ability to see and hear it.

The comfort in knowing that the soul lives on may be clouded by our inability to comprehend fully the concept of life beyond the physical realm. We may have disconcerting questions and concerns about the quality of the soul's existence and experience in the next world: How is my beloved one faring in the next world? Has he come to harm? Is she in pain? What is it like for a soul to be "deprived" of a physical existence?

In the letter written to the aforementioned family from Milan, the Rebbe described the soul's experience when it departs this world:

> Needless to say, insofar as the soul is concerned, it is a release from its "imprisonment" in the body. For so long as [the soul] is bound up with the body, it suffers from physical limitations of the body, which necessarily constrain the soul and involve it in physical activities that are essentially

alien to its purely spiritual nature.… In other words, the departure of the soul from the body is a great advantage and ascent for the soul.[10]

Elsewhere, the Rebbe continues this theme:

Henceforth, the soul is free to enjoy the spiritual bliss of being near to G-d in the fullest measure. That is surely a comforting thought![11]

In these and numerous other communications, the Rebbe echoes the words of the great 12th-century Jewish philosopher Maimonides:

Just as the blind cannot see the spectrum of colors and the deaf cannot hear sound, so too, the mortal body cannot understand the spiritual joys (attained in the Hereafter), which are eternal. These joys have nothing in common with the happiness derived from material things. The essential nature of this heavenly bliss lies in the perception of the essence of the Creator…in the Hereafter, where our souls become wise with the knowledge of G-d. Presently, this joy is unknowable and completely beyond description. There is nothing in our experience that compares to it. For us mortal creatures, it is merely possible to speak of it in the words of the prophet, which express the wonder of this eternal joy: "How[12] abundant is Your goodness!"[13]

CHAPTER 3

SOUL CONNECTION

Certainly, it is a source of comfort to know that the soul lives on and enjoys a state of freedom and goodness far beyond what can be experienced in the physical state. But what about the bond between the bereaved and the departed loved one? Has not that bond been severed? Even if there is a measure of comfort in knowing that one's loved one is in a "better place," how does one deal with the devastating void of a relationship that no longer exists?

Throughout his correspondence with those in mourning, the Rebbe insisted that there remains an ongoing, spiritual connection between the living and the deceased and that this relationship is not merely theoretical, but tangible. It is a dynamic relationship that can be developed and enhanced. In a letter written by the Rebbe to a war widow, he writes:

The ties between two people, and certainly those

between a husband and wife or between parents and children, are chiefly of a spiritual, not of a material, nature. That means that a bullet, a grenade, or a disease can affect the body, but not the spirit or the soul. The physical bond between two persons can be broken…but not their spiritual relationship.[14]

The Rebbe's teachings in this regard come to life in the following story, related by Rabbi Nachum Rabinowitz, a chasid from Jerusalem.[15]

Reb Nachum was once waiting for a private audience with the Rebbe. Among those waiting with him was a man, obviously wealthy, who looked utterly despondent. But when the man emerged from the Rebbe's room, he looked like a different person; his face radiated vitality and optimism.

Curious about this radical change of mood, Reb Nachum inquired about the man's identity from the Rebbe's secretaries and arranged to see him. When the two men met, Reb Nachum asked if the man could share with him what had transpired in the Rebbe's room.

"Recently," the man related, "my only son died. At that point, I felt that my life no longer had any purpose. I saw no value in my wealth and status. I went to see the Rebbe in search of consolation and advice. The Rebbe asked me what my feelings would be if my son went overseas and were living in a foreign country from which he could not communicate with me; however, I could be assured that all his needs were being met and that he wasn't suffering at all. I answered that, although the separation would be difficult to bear, I would be happy for my son."

The Rebbe had continued: "And although he could not respond, if you could communicate to him and send him packages, would you do so?"

The man answered, "Of course."

"This is precisely your present situation," the Rebbe concluded. "With every prayer you recite, you are sending a message to your son. And with every gift you make to charity or institution you fund, you are sending a 'package' to him. He cannot respond, but he appreciates your words and your gifts."

Similarly, when Rabbi Mordechai and Freida Sufrin visited the Rebbe, seeking his comfort after their newborn child had suddenly passed away, the Rebbe said to them: "You should know that while you cannot see your son any longer, he sees you…."

In a compassionate letter written to the grieving teenage daughter of Mrs. Rasha Gansbourg, a young mother who had passed away suddenly on the second day of Sukkot, 1969, the Rebbe explained that through performing good deeds in her mother's merit, especially those inspired by her mother's influence, she and her siblings were not only reaching out to their mother in the next world, or "sending her packages," but were actually enabling her to have a continued presence and impact in the physical world:

> The bond between the living and the soul who has ascended endures, for the soul is enduring and eternal and sees and observes what is taking place with those connected with her and close to her. Every good deed they do causes her spiritual pleasure, specifically the accomplishments of those she has educated and raised in the manner that brings about the said good deeds; that is to say, she has a part in the deeds that result from the education she provided her children and those whom she influenced.[16]

In his letter to the young Ms. Gansbourg, the Rebbe goes on to cite a teaching from *Ethics of the Fathers* that describes both the advantage and the disadvantage for the soul when it departs from the physical world:

> One moment of repentance and good deeds in this world is preferable to the entire World to Come. And one moment of satisfaction in the World to Come is preferable to an entire lifetime in this world.[17]

Therefore, in addition to celebrating its liberation from the body, the soul simultaneously experiences a sense of mourning, realizing she could have ascended even higher by remaining in this world. In this, the soul is comforted and aided by its loved ones who perform good deeds on its behalf in this world.

Similarly, in his letter to Ariel Sharon the Rebbe writes:

> Every positive deed that is directed in accordance with the will of the giver of life, namely G-d, blessed be He, contributes to the pleasure of the soul [of the departed], to its merit, and to its benefit.[18]

In a different letter, the Rebbe elaborates on this theme:

> The departure of the soul from the body is a great advantage and ascent for the soul…the loss is only for the bereaved, and to that extent it is also painful for the soul, of course.
>
> There is yet another point that causes pain to the soul after departing from the body. While the soul is "clothed" in the body, it can actively participate with the body in all matters of Torah, *mitzvot*, and good deeds practiced in the daily life here on earth. But since all this involves physical action and tangible objects, the soul can no

longer engage in these activities when it returns to its heavenly abode, where it can only enjoy the fruits of the Torah, *mitzvot,* and good deeds performed by it in its sojourn on earth. Henceforth, the soul must depend on its relatives and friends to do *mitzvot* and good deeds also on its behalf, and this is the source of true gratification for the soul and helps it ascend to even greater heights.[19]

At a gathering on August 9, 1982, commemorating his father's anniversary of passing, the Rebbe elaborated on this point:

When it comes to a yahrzeit (anniversary of passing), [we recall] the soul of the deceased in the World of Truth, who has come to know the greatness of what can only be accomplished in this physical world. Concerning the study of Torah, the verse declares, "It [the Torah] is not in the Heavens." The Alter Rebbe explains this to mean that any development or resolution of a Torah impasse, or the rendering of a Halachic ruling, can only be accomplished by a physical human being here below.

Likewise, in regards to *mitzvot,* which cannot be performed in the World to Come, since the idea of a mitzvah is to connect a physical object in this world with the spiritual, turning it into an agent of G-dliness in our physical world....

From this it is understood that after passing,

the soul of the deceased finds itself in a state where it requires the actions of those in this world, who have an opportunity to act as agents for the soul to perform these physical deeds, through their physical limbs and organs...on its behalf, and in its merit....[20]

In a letter written to Mrs. Fradel Zilberstrom, the mother of a high school teacher who was murdered in a terrorist attack in Kfar Chabad, Israel, in 1956,[21] the Rebbe conveyed a similar message:

I was notified today that the cornerstone was laid for the new school to be built in Kfar Chabad (in memory of those who were murdered, may their blood be avenged), and I was pleased to hear that you were present and participated in the event. As a woman of faith, you surely know that the soul is a part of G-d and therefore endures eternally. Since the purpose of any soul's descent into a body is for the purpose of elevating this physical world, it emerges that when one connects the departed soul with a physical endeavor, this is the way the soul defies death, so to speak (as it continues to impact the physical world), and this gives the soul immeasurable delight.[22]

Shortly after the Six-Day War, the Rebbe instructed his followers in Israel to arrange care for the orphans and widows of Israel's fallen soldiers. He later wrote of the importance of such work, that their fathers are looking down from heaven; they would like to see their families and children being taken care of. The greatest thing for the fallen soldiers is to be certain that their children grow up as good people.[23]

The good deeds performed by those in mourning can be a source of comfort to the bereaved, filling the void left by death with positive action. But they also provide comfort and pleasure to the departed soul, giving the bereaved family and friends a way to maintain an ongoing, even active, relationship with their loved ones.

CHAPTER 4
A TIME FOR MOURNING

Should these points of consolation be taken to the other extreme and eliminate mourning altogether? Indeed, if the soul experiences relief in its release from the body and the freedom to experience unadulterated spiritual bliss, what place is there for grief? Perhaps expressions of grief even indicate a lack of belief in the eternality of the soul and in the perfection of G-d's ways?

The Rebbe saw the answer to these questions in the Torah's laws of mourning:

> It may be asked: If [death] is a "release" for the soul, why has the Torah prescribed periods of mourning, etc.? But there is really no contradiction. The Torah recognizes the natural feeling of grief that is felt by the loss of a near and dear one, whose passing leaves a void in the family, and the physical presence and contact of the beloved one will be sorely missed. So the Torah has prescribed the proper periods of mourning to give expression

to these feelings and to make it easier to regain the proper equilibrium and adjustment.[24]

Elsewhere, the Rebbe similarly writes:

> Nevertheless, the departure and ascent of the soul to its Heavenly abode is mourned for a time by the surviving relatives and friends, because the person is no longer *physically* here on earth and can no longer be seen, heard, and felt by the physical senses and is therefore sadly missed.[25]

The Rebbe saw the Torah's teachings, and the way they are implemented into practical law, as a prescription to ease our suffering in the face of pain but also as addressing the truth of human nature. The stages of mourning outlined in Jewish law provide the appropriate framework for the mourner, in which he or she can express grief and process the loss in stages as time progresses.

But the Rebbe would also stress how the selfsame mourning practices and rituals that validate the mourner's grief and facilitate its expression also provide the mechanism by which to gradually move beyond it:

> Every Jew has been instructed by the Creator and Master of the world that the matters connected with *avelut* (mourning) must be limited in time, though during the proper time it is natural and

proper to give vent to one's pain and sorrow at the sad loss in keeping with the nature which G-d implanted in man.

However, when the various periods of mourning pass—the first three days of profound grief and tears, the seven days of *shivah*, [the thirty days of] *sheloshim*, etc.—then it is not permitted to extend these periods beyond their allotted days. And since this is the instruction of the Creator and Master of the world, it is clear that carrying out these Divine instructions is within the capability of every Jew, for G-d does not expect the impossible of His creatures and provides everyone beforehand with the necessary capacity and strength to carry out its instructions as set forth in His Torah, called *Torat Emet* ("Torah of truth"), because it is true and realistic in all its teachings and imperatives.[26]

Sometimes mourners find it hard to let go of their grief. As the traditional seven-day mourning period comes to an end, the mourner might wonder: "Isn't it callous of me to return to normal living so soon after losing someone so dear to me?" Or: "If I really cared about my loved one, wouldn't I still be overwhelmed with grief?" And perhaps most devastating of all: "Is it not an insult to the soul that its departure from life on earth is being 'gotten over' by its loved ones?"

The Rebbe's response to such thoughts was emphatic:

> Those who think that the gradual lessening of mourning may cause the soul of the departed to feel slighted are totally wrong. The very opposite is true: Excessive mourning by relatives is not good for the soul in the World of Truth.[27]

Indeed, the Rebbe would insist that not only is it not selfish or insensitive to limit one's grief, but by over-extending the mourning period, one is in fact placing one's own interests before those of the deceased. The Rebbe writes:

> To allow oneself to be carried away by these feelings [of sorrow] beyond the limits set by the Torah—in addition to it being a disservice to one's self and all around, as well as to the soul of the departed, as mentioned above—would mean that one is more concerned with one's own feelings than with the feelings of the dear soul that has risen to new spiritual heights of eternal happiness. Thus, paradoxically, the overextended feeling of grief, which is due to the great love for the departed one, actually causes pain to the loved one, since the soul continues to take an interest in the dear one left behind, sees what is going on (even better than before), rejoices with them in their joys, etc.[28]

In a letter written in 1975 to Mrs. Rose Goldfield, who tragically lost her son in a car accident, the Rebbe took the notion of limiting grief for the sake of the departed soul even further. In his letter he pointed out that not only does the departed soul want its loved ones to move beyond their grief and live life to the fullest, it desires that they do so not out of a sense of burdensome obligation but with inner peace and joy.

> ...It follows that when a close person passes on, by the will of G-d, those left here can no longer see him with their eyes or hear him with their ears; but the soul, in the World of Truth, can see and hear. And when he sees that the relatives are overly disturbed by his physical absence, it is saddened, and, conversely, when it sees that after the mourning period prescribed by the Torah a normal and fully productive life is resumed, it can happily rest in peace.
>
> ...It is possible to enlarge upon the above, but knowing your family background and tradition, I trust the above will suffice. I might add, however, that one must beware of the Yetzer-hara (one's Base Inclination) who is very crafty and knows that certain people cannot be approached openly and without disguise. So he tries to trick them by disguising himself in a mantle of piety and emotionalism, etc., saying: You know, G-d has prescribed a period of mourning, which shows

that it is the right thing to do; so why not do more than that and extend the period? In this way he may have a chance to succeed in distracting the person from the fact that at the end of the said period, the Torah requires the Jew to serve G-d with joy. The Yetzer-hara will even encourage a person to give Tzedoko (charity) in memory of the soul, except that in each case it be associated with sadness and pain. But, as indicated, this is exactly contrary to the objective, which is to cause pleasure and gratification to the soul.

May G-d grant that, inasmuch as we are approaching the Festival of Our Freedom, including also freedom from everything that distracts a Jew from serving G-d wholeheartedly and with joy, that this should be so also with you, in the midst of all our people, and that you should be a source of inspiration and strength to your husband, children and grandchildren, and all around you.

It was not enough for the Rebbe to simply state the principle that excessive mourning is detrimental, both to oneself and to the departed soul. As the following two examples demonstrate, he often gave detailed, practical guidance on how to achieve the aim of moving on after a loss.

A couple, utterly broken after the death of their adolescent daughter, came to the Rebbe to seek advice. While they were financially and socially comfortable in their community, remaining in a place that continually reminded them of their daughter meant that they were continually reliving the trauma of her loss. They were contemplating moving their family to a new place, hoping that would allow them to heal.

"Your other children," the Rebbe asked, "where can you best raise them with love?" The couple, unsure how to respond, listened closely as the Rebbe continued. "If moving will open your hearts to healing and allow your family to flourish as it should, do not fear the challenges a new place will bring. Follow the path that will nourish your other children. They need to live with love."[29]

Sometimes, moving on requires leaving the past behind to focus on the love that exists in the present. But sometimes, moving on might require first facing the past head-on.

"I can't stop living in the past," a Holocaust survivor once confided in the Rebbe. "A dark shadow constantly hangs over my life, and I can't help but view life through the prism of my traumatic past."

"Have you ever spoken about your experiences?" the Rebbe asked gently.

"No, I haven't," the gentleman responded, "I find it too painful."

"Then I suggest you write a memoir," the Rebbe

advised, "but make sure to write it yourself, not through a ghostwriter."[30]

There was one occasion on which the Rebbe shared with his followers how the Torah-ordained vehicles for expressing grief and processing loss had become a reality for him in his own personal life.

The occasion was a talk given by the Rebbe in his home on the eve of the 22nd of Adar 5748 (March 10, 1988). Those who were present at the talk, and the thousands who listened to it via telephone hookup at numerous locations worldwide, will never forget that evening.

Just thirty days prior, the Rebbe had suffered the loss of his wife, Rebbetzin Chaya Mushka Schneerson, of blessed memory. Married for fifty-nine years, they had survived Stalin's Russia, escaped Hitler's Berlin and Nazi-occupied France, and lived childless together for 47 years in the United States.

Her sudden passing, in the middle of the night, while visiting the hospital due to an ulcer, profoundly affected the Rebbe. During the funeral and initial period of mourning, the Rebbe's intense grief was apparent. But the first time he spoke publicly about his emotions was thirty days after her passing at a weeknight talk from his home on President Street in Brooklyn.

The Rebbe began his talk by noting the "milestones" which Torah law establishes for the process of mourning a loved one. There is the intense mourning of the first three days following the burial (characterized as a time for "weeping"); the seven-day mourning period (*shivah*); the mourning practices of the first thirty days (*sheloshim*); and the practices (including the recitation of *kaddish*) of the first year. Torah law *obligates* us to mourn, yet also obligates us to decrease the intensity of our mourning at each of these stages.

The Rebbe then cited an enigmatic Midrash which describes an exchange between G-d and Moses. G-d was conveying to Moses the laws governing various states of ritual impurity and how one achieves purification from them. When mention was made of the impurity brought on through physical contact with a dead body, Moses blanched and asked, "G-d Almighty, but how can one be cleansed of this impurity?"

While the exchange between G-d and Moses seems strictly legal in nature, a deeper reading reveals the conversation to be deeply philosophical and existential as well. What Moses was really asking was: How can the devastating void created by death ever be filled? How can the numbing and lifeless sensation that such loss brings ever be healed or "purified"?

Now, Moses was a man of deep faith in G-d and His ways, and he certainly understood what the Torah has to say about the process of purification following contact with death. Why, asked the Rebbe, did he have such a visceral reaction particularly to this law? But Moses' "question" was not a rational one. Intellectually, he grasped all of the logical and spiritual explanations on the issue of death. But upon perceiving the unbearable sorrow that accompanies death, he cried out to G-d: But how can one reconcile an understanding mind with a bleeding heart? How can the painful residual effects of death ever be healed by a legal and ritualistic process?

The Rebbe then applied this outcry to his own situation. The mind understands the difference between the first three days and the *shivah*, between the *shivah* and the *sheloshim*, and between the *sheloshim* and the first year; but the heart does not accept it. As we reach each of these milestones, we know that it is our duty to move on to the next phase of the mourning process, but we find it very difficult to do so. One need not be disheartened by this: the Midrash tells us that Moses himself could not immediately prevail upon his heart to feel what his mind had been given to understand. Even after G-d revealed the ritualistic process by which one can be cleansed from the taint of death, it remains a *chok*, a suprarational "decree." Yet G-d commands us to make these transitions, and He empowers us to fulfill His command.

Therefore, we must do everything in our power to integrate our knowledge and emotions, both in order to function well in our own lives and for the sake of our work on behalf of others as well. For surely, those who are dependent upon us cannot be made to wait until our minds and hearts have fully integrated what we know to be expected of us! And the power of the divine decree is such that we can ultimately prevail upon ourselves to sublimate the negativities of death.[31]

It was clear to all present that the Rebbe's words, spoken with such intensity and emotion, were autobiographical, born out of his own recent encounter with loss.

CHAPTER 5

DON'T DESPAIR

Upon losing someone near and dear, there will often be moments when the grief will seem too much to bear. "There is only so much pain I can handle," the mourner might say to him- or herself before collapsing and falling into dysfunction.

What follows is a moving account shared by Mr. Yaakov Schiffman about the Rebbe's personal involvement and encouragement at a very difficult time in his life, which helped lift him out of despair when all seemed lost.

In 1973, which was the year that I celebrated my bar mitzvah, my parents sent me to a summer camp in Israel. When I came back, I learned that my father was about to undergo surgery. It turned out he had colon cancer, and from that point on his health went downhill.

Two years later, just before the holiday of *Purim*, my father's condition took a turn for the worse. We went to the hospital, and after the doctors examined him they called me in and said, "You'd better go home; your father is staying here tonight." That night the doctors operated on him and found that there wasn't much they could do but try to make the end as painless as possible.

Of course, we didn't want to give up, so we went to several rabbis for blessings. We even tried the alternative medicines of the time. My father lost a lot of weight, and nothing seemed to be working. Then one of our relatives told us, "You should go to see the Lubavitcher Rebbe."

It was wintertime when we went to see the Rebbe. There were five of us at that meeting: my father and mother, my grandmother, my sister, and me. My father was so ill; he was haggard, and his face had lost its glow.

We entered the Rebbe's office. I stood in the back of the room, and my father spoke quietly with the Rebbe for a few minutes. When the Rebbe finished speaking with my father, we began to leave, when suddenly the Rebbe said to me, "You stay."

I was already anxious with everything that was going on; I was only sixteen years old at the time, and I became very nervous.

The Rebbe gently said to me, "Come over here," gesturing that I should approach. He went over to his shelf and pulled out two volumes of the Talmud, and he said to me in Yiddish:

"By the laws of medicine, your father is extremely sick now; he's near the end. G-d will help, but your father will be depressed, and you're going to be depressed. You'll need something to give you strength. I want to teach you something which will help keep you going."

He opened up to page 10a of Tractate *Berachot* and began to teach me the story from II Kings [20:1-6] that the Talmud is discussing. King Hezekiah was ill, and the Prophet Isaiah visited him. The prophet told the king that his days were numbered and he should prepare to die, but Hezekiah refused to accept this and said, "No, I have faith in G-d." Although the prophet said it was too late, Hezekiah began to pray because, "even if the tip of the sword is pointed at your throat, you should never give up hope."

I was standing across the desk from the Rebbe, and he was sitting. But in middle of the story, the Rebbe motioned for me to come around the desk, and I looked into the volume together with him. He translated the dialog slowly into Yiddish, word by word, pointing to the place, the way a father teaches his son.

I remember him pointing to the words with his finger, then looking at me, and pointing again. He had me repeat it until it was clear that I understood. Though my father was quite knowledgeable in the Talmud, the Rebbe wanted to make sure that I understood the Talmud's idea well and that I could explain it to my father, as well. The idea he kept stressing was that even at death's door you should never give up hope, you should never become depressed, and you should accept G-d's will. It took quite some time—about twenty-five minutes.

What stands out in my mind more than anything else is the earnest, loving way the Rebbe looked at me. I never saw that type of love. Here I was, a stranger to him, a young boy coming with his father, who needed a blessing. He gave his blessing, but then he gave much more. He saw that this boy needed fatherly love, and he gave it.

When I came out of the Rebbe's office, I was sweating. As we drove home, I told my father what had happened, and he broke down and cried. As soon as we got home, we learned the piece at least three or four times.

I remember that my father asked me a few times, "Do you understand why the Rebbe told you to learn this with me? Do you understand?"

Two and a half months after our visit with the Rebbe, my father passed away. It was Monday night, the

18th of Shevat, and the last thing he said to me was that I had made him very proud and had given him tremendous nachas.

After he passed away, I was on the verge of becoming despondent. I didn't have relatives to look after me—my mother was an only child, and my father's whole family had been wiped out in the war—and I was only sixteen years old.

I don't know how to thank the Rebbe for this fact, but he sat me down and told me the facts of life. Everyone else had been telling me, "No, it'll be good; it'll be good." The Rebbe looked at me and told me how to be prepared for it.

I had times when things got tough. I left my studies for a while and wandered away. But then I remembered what the Rebbe taught me. Through those years, I probably learned that piece of the Talmud thirty times, and it got me back on track.

The fact that I am an observant Jew and that I raised a beautiful family is because of that day when the Rebbe spent so much time with me and explained to me: When you have a problem and are feeling that you've hit rock bottom, remember never to give up, because G-d is there. Open your heart to Him, and He will help you.[32]

The knowledge that there is a constant Higher force in our lives that is intimately involved in and deeply concerned with our well-being enables us to overcome our darkest moments. When we encounter low points in life, reflecting on G-d's continuous presence in our lives helps provide us with the comfort and confidence it takes to replace despair with hope and empowers us to look forward to and prepare for a better tomorrow.

CHAPTER 6

THE STRENGTH TO PREVAIL

In difficult moments, many have found encouragement in a pivotal and inspiring teaching of the Rebbe, based on the words of Talmud,[33] "G-d does not make impossible demands on His creations."

Just as it is inconceivable that loving parents would knowingly give their child a task that is beyond their capabilities, G-d, our loving Parent, does not present us with a challenge that is beyond our capacity to meet.

The Rebbe took this idea a step further, teaching that the greater the challenge we face in life, *the greater is the accompanying inner strength we possess* in order to overcome the challenge. As the following story demonstrates, in the Rebbe's worldview, challenges of any kind are indicative of inner strength, not weakness.

A traditional Jew who found himself in a relationship forbidden by the Torah once visited the Rebbe to discuss his religious quandary.

After presenting his situation to the Rebbe, the man fell silent. He braced himself for a rebuke, expecting to be told how grave a transgression he was committing.

The Rebbe was silent for a little while. "I envy you," he finally said.

The young man did not quite grasp the meaning. "The Rebbe," he thought, "who is on the highest of spiritual planes, is envious of *me?*"

The Rebbe continued: "There are many ladders in life; each person is given his or her own. The ladders present themselves as life's challenges and difficult choices. The tests you face are the ladders that elevate you to great heights—the greater the challenge, the higher the ladder.

"G-d has given you this difficult test because He believes you can overcome it and has endowed you with the ability to do so. Only the strongest are presented a ladder as challenging as yours.

"Don't you see, then, why I envy you?"[34]

Along similar lines, the Rebbe wrote the following lines to a young man who wrote to him describing the difficult moral and religious dilemma he faced:

> By the Grace of G-d
> 25th of Shevat, 5746 [February 4, 1986]
> Brooklyn, N. Y.

Greeting and Blessing:

This is to acknowledge receipt of your letter of Jan. 26th, in which you write about a serious problem.

As requested, I will remember you in prayer for the fulfillment of your heart's desires for good....

Needless to say, a person who is afflicted with this or other neurological problems may well ask, "Why has G-d created such a compulsive drive, one that is in direct contradiction to His moral Code? Why has he afflicted me, who desires to comply fully with His commandments?"

No human being can answer such questions, which only G-d, the Creator, can answer. One observation that can be suggested in relation to the question "Why me?": If an individual experiences a particularly difficult, or trying, situation, it may be assumed that G-d has given him extraordinary powers to overcome the extraordinary difficulty. The individual concerned is probably unaware of his real inner strength; the trial may therefore be designed for the sole purpose of bringing out in the individual his hidden strength, which, after overcoming his problem, can be added henceforth to the arsenal of his revealed capacities in order to utilize both for infinitely greater achievements for the benefit of himself and others.

[Maimonides, the "Guide of the Perplexed" of

his generation and of all subsequent generations, who was also acclaimed as the greatest physician of his time, declares in a well-known passage in his famous Code, Mishneh Torah (Yad Hachazaka): "Every person has the option (power), if he so desires, to direct himself to do only good and be a tzaddik, or, if he chooses, to follow the bad road and be a rasha. Do not ever think that a person is predestined from birth to be a tzaddik or rasha. Nor is there any inner compulsion to make a choice, but one has the capacity to choose the right behavior, and it is entirely a matter of one's own will and determination" (Free translation from Hil. Teshuvah, Ch. 5. See it there at length.)]

As the Rebbe made clear on many occasions,[35] the idea that G-d does not give human beings greater challenges than they can handle applies to all of life's challenges, not just moral and religious ones.

In the summer of 1976, the Israeli Defense Forces sponsored a tour of the United States for a large group of disabled veterans. While they were in New York, a Lubavitcher chasid came to their hotel and suggested that they meet with the Rebbe. When the group accepted the invitation, arrangements were quickly made to transport them (many of them were wheelchair bound) to the Rebbe's headquarters. Soon they found ourselves in the famous large synagogue in the basement of 770 Eastern Parkway.

After apologizing to the group for his Ashkenazic-accented Hebrew, the Rebbe delivered a short address, in which he said: "If a person has been deprived of a limb or a faculty, this itself indicates that G-d has given him special powers to overcome the limitations this entails and to surpass the achievements of ordinary people. You are not 'disabled' or 'handicapped,' but special and unique, as you possess potentials that the rest of us do not."

"I therefore suggest," the Rebbe continued, adding with a smile, "of course it is none of my business, but Jews are famous for voicing opinions on matters that do not concern them—that you should no longer be called *nechei Yisrael* ('the disabled of Israel,' their official designation by the IDF) but *metzuyanei Yisrael* ('the special of Israel')."[36]

After delivering his address, the Rebbe walked among the group, going from wheelchair to wheelchair, shaking their hands and adding a personal word or two to each. He also gave each a dollar bill to contribute to charity on his behalf, making them his partners in the fulfillment of a mitzvah.

It was the Rebbe's staunch and empowering belief

that all challenges, as impossible and insurmountable as they may seem, are accompanied by a commensurate reservoir of fortitude and inner strength, empowering us to reach deeper into ourselves and muster the courage and conviction necessary to forge ahead on our life's journey. The Rebbe taught that a challenge is a calling and that the tribulations sprinkled throughout our lives are there in order to bring us into closer contact with our deeper or higher selves.

CHAPTER 7

RESPECTING THE WISHES OF THE DEPARTED

The Rebbe taught that the souls of departed loved ones are actually still involved in the lives of those they leave on earth.

Shortly after the Six-Day War, the Rebbe instructed his followers in Israel to arrange care for the orphans and widows of Israel's fallen soldiers. He later wrote of the importance of such work: "Their fathers…are looking down from heaven; they would like to see their families and children being taken care of. The greatest thing for the fallen soldiers is to be certain that their children grow up as good people."[37]

This continued interest in the lives of the living includes not only an interest in spiritual or religious matters but also in the everyday joys and challenges of life. From a letter of the Rebbe:

> The soul itself retains all its faculties and, as

explained in our holy sources, reacts to the conduct and feelings of its relatives left behind, sharing in their joys and in their sorrows…and it prays and intercedes on behalf of its relatives here on earth.[38]

The Rebbe expresses this idea in another letter, written to a woman who lost one of her sons prematurely after having been informed that her older son had become reclusive from grief:

Since your son's withdrawn condition is the result of what happened to his brother, explain to him gently that, per our belief, the soul is eternal and remains connected to its family [and that] his sadness and seclusion will not bring his beloved brother pleasure.[39]

As the following anecdotes illustrate, the Rebbe would often encourage people to take into account the interests and pastimes of those who had passed on.

When Rabbi Moshe Feller, who is today the senior Chabad emissary in Minnesota, was twenty-four years old, his mother passed away. A few years later, the Rebbe asked Rabbi Dovid Raskin to suggest a match between Feller's father and a widow named Mrs. Gross. The two ended up meeting and decided to get married. Before the wedding, the Rebbe sent Moshe Feller an

unsolicited note. Knowing that he may have been both-
ered by another woman becoming his father's wife, the
Rebbe wrote the following to him (paraphrased): "You
should know that by remarrying, your father will bring
happiness to your mother, of blessed memory, since he
will now have a life companion who can help take care
of him, and this is what she would have wanted."[40]

In his thoughtful note to the young Rabbi Feller, the
Rebbe addressed a painful concern that often plagues
children of a deceased parent whose other parent is
contemplating marriage to a new spouse.

"Won't this hurt the soul of my departed parent?"
they may wonder. "Won't Mother or Father feel slighted, or even envious, if their former life's partner creates
a new life with a new spouse?"

The Rebbe's note to Feller taught, in effect, that once
a soul disengages from its physical body and environ-
ment, it is freed of all human weaknesses that once col-
ored its perceptions and feelings while on earth. As the
soul is no longer governed or affected by the petty and
self-centered insecurities which stem from the human
condition, it is free to experience unadulterated joy in
the well-being of its loved ones below.

Each Sukkot, Rabbi Berel and Esther Raskin would
invite the Lubavitch community of Crown Heights,

Brooklyn, where they lived, to their *sukkah* to partake in a lavish *kiddush* and a holiday get-together. In the year after Esther's father, Rabbi Yankel Lispker, passed away, she didn't feel it was appropriate to host this festive and spirited gathering. When the Rebbe heard that there might not be a *kiddush* at the Raskins that year he said, "On the contrary! Reb Yankel, who is currently in *Gan Eden* ("Paradise"), will come visit your *sukkah*, as was his custom while alive, and no one will be there saying *l'chaim*. Not only should there be a *kiddush* this year, there should a larger *kiddush* than usual!"[41]

The Rebbe himself had occasion to practice this principle when it came to the loss of his own beloved wife, Rebbetzin Chaya Mushka.

Dr. Robert Feldman, who was one of the Rebbetzin's physicians, enjoyed close relations with her and would often visit with her. Shortly before the Rebbetzin's passing, Dr. Feldman's daughter, Sarah, became engaged to her future husband, Levi Shemtov. The Rebbetzin, who had offered Sarah motherly advice while she was dating, was delighted with the news. The couple-to-be planned to visit the Rebbetzin together, but she passed away before the visit could take place.

Right after *shivah*, the seven-day mourning period

for the Rebbetzin, the Rebbe sent for Dr. Feldman. "Tell me, when is the engagement party?" he asked.

That wasn't a simple question to answer. According to the original plan, the party was scheduled to take place within the first thirty days of the Rebbetzin's passing, considered by Jewish law to be a period of mourning. However, to push off a happy occasion was no small matter either. Before Dr. Feldman could answer, the Rebbe continued: "It should take place on the day it was originally scheduled for, and it should not be smaller than originally planned. In fact, it should be bigger!"

The Feldmans had been planning a small party in their home. But the Rebbe insisted that the celebration be held in a rented hall, with live music, and the food should be served on china, "and the main thing: much joy!" The Rebbe's tone then softened, and in a voice filled with emotion he said, "It should be done this way because this is how the Rebbetzin would have wanted it to be…and this is what will make the Rebbetzin happy."[42]

The Rebbe's approach was that, whenever possible, happy occasions of those peripherally connected to a tragedy should not be aborted or pushed off. On the contrary, extra effort should be made to increase the joy, as that is what the deceased would have wanted.

CHAPTER 8

MISPLACED GUILT

"Was this tragedy my fault? Had I done things different-
ly, could I have averted catastrophe?"

These and similar questions can endlessly haunt the
relatives or caretakers of someone who died an untimely death. Hypothetical "if only" scenarios and endless
imaginings of better endings are especially destructive.
Such second-guessing disrupts peace of mind and causes
feelings of guilt, which can drain whatever energy is left
in those already suffering terribly from loss.

Responsible and loving family members and caregiv-
ers need to be confident in the knowledge that they did
all in their power to help their loved one and that the
rest was beyond their control.

This was the approach that the Rebbe advocated, as
the following letter indicates. The addressee had written
the Rebbe regarding a tragic event that had occurred in
his home. He had invited members of his community
to a festive meal on Shavuot to celebrate the completion

of a Torah scroll, which was scheduled to be presented to a synagogue in a few days. During the course of the celebration, a young woman suddenly fell ill and died. The Rebbe responded:

> Each and every individual has been granted a set amount of years of life on earth. It is only in extreme cases that one's deeds can lengthen or shorten them with some terrible sin, etc., G-d forbid.[43]

This belief is absolutely essential to dispelling unjustified feelings of culpability, and it is wholly supported by the Torah. Indeed, the idea that no one passes away before his time is alluded to in the opening verse of the Torah portion *Chayei Sarah*: "Sarah's lifetime was one hundred years, and twenty years, and seven years; the years of Sarah's life."[44]

The obvious curiosity in this verse is the seeming redundancy of its final words: "the years of Sara's life." According to the Midrash, the circumstances surrounding Sarah's passing—"she heard the news that her son... was nearly slaughtered, and her soul flew from her"[45]— might be perceived as the *cause* of her death, when, in fact, the reason for her death was that these 127 years were "the years of Sarah's life"—i.e., the exact amount of time prescribed for her by G-d.

There is a profound lesson here. Sometimes we attribute certain results, positive or negative, to unexpected circumstances we encounter in life. For example, a couple experiencing difficulty having children for an extended period of time might one day seek the counsel of a new doctor and then have a child soon after. They may say to themselves, if only we had visited this doctor sooner, we would have averted all the heartache of our childless years.

However, from a spiritual perspective, the reality is very different: For reasons known only to G-d, this couple was destined to be childless for a determined period of time. When that period was over, the agent chosen by G-d to facilitate the birth of their child was this particular doctor they heard about at this particular time.

And the same is true of tragic occurrences that cause the loss of life. If someone is struck by a car and dies as a result, it is only natural to think that the cause of death was the car accident and to speculate that if the deceased had shown up a minute sooner or later, he or she might still be alive. These thoughts are not only terribly painful, they are also untrue, for in actual fact, the time for the deceased to pass on had come, and the car accident was simply the facilitator of their passing.

Recognizing and internalizing the belief that each

person has an allotted time on earth, and we cannot add to or subtract from that amount of time, can help us let go of unnecessary guilt and attain a certain measure of inner peace.

CHAPTER 9

LOSING A CHILD

The greatest tragedy a parent can experience is the loss of a child. Especially when the death is the result of a sudden, tragic event, the searing pain of loss and the unanswerable questions that result from it torment the parents and family of the child.

On the eve of Passover, 1988, a six-year-old girl named Miriam Gaerman was killed in a car accident in Berkeley, California. Following her death, her parents wrote a long letter to the Rebbe, seeking some kind of explanation for this tragic event. They were particularly distressed by the feeling that their daughter's untimely passing meant that she did not have a chance to fulfill her role on earth. They also felt that they did not have an opportunity to mourn her properly, because, according to Jewish law, the festival of Passover ended the *shivah* mourning period (usually observed for one week) after only a few hours.

The Rebbe responded to both their concerns:

It goes without saying that no one can possibly interpret the ways of G-d with any degree of certainty....

[That said,] all souls that come down at this time [of history] are continuing previous incarnations in order to complete (totally or partially) what they did not complete previously. And [even though, generally speaking, man is meant to live 70, 80 years,[46] etc.], those who pass on [at a young age,] before their obligation to fulfill the commandments, came into this world [only] to finish the number of years that they lacked....

If Miriam needed to finish the number of years she lacked in this world and then go immediately into Paradise, her parents should try not to be saddened, but take comfort in the knowledge that on this Passover she was in *Gan Eden*. And for this reason, they could find true joy on the holy day, according to the Torah of Truth.[47]

There is a famous Chasidic story that exemplifies this concept of a short life lived in order to complete a rectification from a previous reincarnation. A couple who had lost their two-year-old son came to the Baal Shem Tov and poured out their hearts to him. The Baal Shem Tov told them that their child had a special soul that had already been in this world. However, it needed to return for a few years in order to achieve a *tikkun*, a rectification. When the *tikkun* was complete, the soul could return to its source.[48]

Along similar lines, a woman who had suffered a number of miscarriages once wrote to the Rebbe seeking his guidance and blessing. The Rebbe responded that there are some souls whose sole mission in this world is to fulfill a deficit remaining from a previous incarnation. In particular, the Rebbe continued, there are some souls that were conceived in circumstances considered by Jewish law to be less than ideal and, in order to achieve spiritual completion, return to this world for the sole purpose of being conceived in purity! Once this brief mission on earth is completed these pure souls return to the World of Truth, having achieved the spiritual perfection they previously lacked.[49]

The Sages of the Talmud dealt with the loss of a child from a different angle. Rather than focusing on considerations of a soul's destiny, they looked at the nature of parenthood itself—and found comfort there. What follows is a discussion between Rabban Yochanan ben Zakkai and his disciples after the loss of his son:

"Comfort me," requested [Rabban Yochanan ben Zakkai] of his disciples.

Rabbi Eliezer spoke up. "Adam lost a son too. Nevertheless, he found consolation."

But Rabban Yochanan only retorted, "Why do you add to my sorrow the sorrow of someone else?"

Rabbi Yehoshua spoke in turn: "Job had sons and daughters, and he lost them all. Nevertheless, he found consolation."

Again Rabban Yochanan only answered, "Why do you add to my sorrow the sorrow of someone else?"

Then Rabbi Yosse said, "Aaron had two exceptional sons who both died on the same day. Yet Aaron was comforted."

This, too, Rabban Yochanan rejected with the same words.

Rabbi Shimon then rose and spoke: "King David lost a son and was nevertheless comforted."

Rabban Yochanan reacted as before.

Then Rabbi Elazar ben Arach spoke: "Allow me to tell you this story: A king entrusted one of his subjects with a precious object to keep safe for him, and the man worried incessantly, for he had to return this object to the king undamaged. Only when he returned the precious thing to the king intact was he relieved of his anxiety. You, my teacher, are in the same situation. You had a son who has left this world without sin. Let it be a consolation that you have returned to G-d in a perfect state what He entrusted to you."

"Elazar, you have comforted me!" Rabban Yochanan said.[50]

Bruria, the wife of Rabbi Meir, adopted the same attitude when her two sons died suddenly on a Shabbat. She laid their bodies in the bedroom, and when her husband came home, she posed to him what appeared to be a question in Jewish law: "A while ago, someone entrusted an object stone to me for safekeeping. Now the owner has come back to reclaim. Should I return it to him?"

Rabbi Meir immediately replied that she must return the precious stone without hesitation. Bruria then led him into the bedroom.[51]

In his book, Rabbi Vorst concludes that this is how he and his wife must look at the tragic loss of their own son: "that we have not been deprived of Boruch; we 'only' gave him back."[52]

This attitude also helped Rabbi Vorst to deal compassionately with the woman whose car struck and killed his son. When she came to the house of *shivah*, he praised her courage and tried to put her at ease by telling her that he did not blame her, since "everything is destined and by Divine Providence foreseen and arranged by G-d."

"Even if she had not driven too fast," Rabbi Vorst

reflects in his book, "Baruch still would not have been with us anymore. For evidently, his time had come."[53]

CHAPTER 10

COMMEMORATING LOVED ONES

One of the ways that we cope with loss is to try to ensure that the memory of our loved ones does not fade. We may seek to keep their memory alive by erecting monuments as tangible reminders of their legacy.

The Rebbe had a very particular view on how best to memorialize our loved ones, as is illustrated in this story:

The Rebbe was once asked for guidance by a family who were looking for an inscription for their deceased father's headstone. The following is a free translation of the Rebbe's response:

> It is obvious that the inscription should be agreed upon by the offspring of the departed. It is beyond doubt that primarily they ought to contemplate the fact that the headstone is a "stone" with wording engraved upon it. However, the offspring of the departed stand as a "living" monument,

and their daily deeds and behavior acts as a living inscription on a living monument. The wording of this kind of inscription depends only upon themselves. In the language of our Sages, "A son is the leg of the father."[54]

On the fourth anniversary of his wife's passing, the Rebbe shared a similar message: "Kaddish is once again recited on this day, and that elevates the soul…particularly [that of] a woman who merited that many Jewish girls carry her name and show a living example, living souls in living bodies, uninterrupted life, [girls that] are educated in her spirit and by her teachings and her example."[55]

The Rebbe made a similar point regarding Machon Chana, an institution for higher learning for girls established in the name and memory of the Rebbe's mother, Rebetzin Chana, of blessed memory.

On numerous occasions, the Rebbe made it clear that there was very special place in his heart for Machon Chana, the first institution he allowed to be named after his beloved mother.

For instance, the Rebbe once told Rabbi and Mrs. Itche Gansberg who were dorm parents at the time: "Thank you for raising my daughters."

On a different occasion the Rebbe insisted that every one of the girls at Machon Chana be provided a

Passover plate made of silver, rather than disposables, so that they feel like royalty as is befitting the "daughters" of his dear mother.

Indeed, the Rebbe made a point of visiting Machon Chana each year on Passover eve, before going home to conduct his own *Seder*, in order to wish the girls well. And one year as he approached the building which housed Machon Chana, the Rebbe said to its co-founder, Rabbi Jacob J. Hecht, "Now I am going home."

The Rebbe explained that since the girls follow in his mother's footsteps, her presence is always found in Machon Chana.[56]

Similarly, during a private audience with the Rebbe in the early 1950s, an influential leader of the Jewish Federation of North America proposed that all Jewish families set up an empty chair at their Passover festive Seder meal to perpetuate the memory of the millions tragically killed in the Holocaust.[57] The Rebbe responded: "Your idea is a nice one, but with all due respect, instead of leaving the chair empty, let us fill that chair with an extra guest. Invite a Jew who would otherwise not participate in a Seder. This would be a true living legacy and a victory for the Jewish nation."

The Rebbe gave similar advice to the Polish-born rabbi, Yechezkel Besser, who made it his mission to preserve abandoned and vandalized Jewish cemeteries in his native country. When he met with Rebbetzin Besser, the Rebbe advised: "Tell your husband, he should also remember the *chaim* ('the living'), not just the *beit hachaim* ('the cemeteries')." Rabbi Besser got the message and, as his biographer Warren Kozak relates in *The Rabbi of 84th Street*, he began to revitalize Jewish life in Poland, bringing kosher food to the country and organizing Torah classes.[58]

Likewise, when the Rebbe's cousin, Yitzchak Schneerson, wrote to him in 1952, telling him of his involvement in Paris in the creation of the Tomb of the Unknown Jewish Martyr, today called Memorial of the Shoah, to memorialize victims of the Holocaust, the Rebbe wrote back politely but forcefully, "Forgive me if my view is not in accordance with yours…. Now at a time when there are hundreds of thousands of living martyrs, not 'unknown' by any stretch, who live in abject need for physical bread, and many more in need of spiritual sustenance, the main impediment to meeting their needs is simply lack of funds. Therefore, whenever funds can be procured, this immediately creates a dilemma: Should the monies be used to erect a stone [memoriam] in a large square in Paris to remind passersby of the millions of Jews who died sanctifying G-d's

Name, or should these monies sustain the living who are starving, either literally or figuratively, to hear the word of G-d? The solution to your dilemma is, I believe, not in doubt."[59]

It should be noted that the Rebbe's life was deeply affected by the Holocaust and he had personally lost numerous family members during the war, including his brother Dov Ber, who was murdered by the Nazis, as were his sister-in-law and brother-in-law, Sheina and Menachem Mendel Horenstein, who were killed at the death camp of Treblinka. The Rebbe mentioned his personal losses in a postscript to a letter he wrote to a child of Holocaust survivors, who had written to him about his struggles with religious doubts:

> "Needless to say, the above may be accepted intellectually…and one may perhaps say, 'Well, it is easy for one who is not emotionally involved to give an "intellectual" explanation….' So I ought, perhaps, to add that I, too, lost in the Holocaust very close and dear relatives such as a grandmother, brother, cousins, and others (may G-d avenge their blood)."[60]

Throughout his talks and correspondence, the Rebbe continually encouraged people to take positive action to create a living legacy rather than a static one, even when the legacy proposed was a holy one.

He did the same when he experienced the loss of his own wife, at which point he repeatedly requested that his wife's legacy be recognized through positive actions.

Indeed, although then Rebbe rarely ventured beyond his home and his office at 770 Eastern Parkway, the Rebbe personally visited the groundbreaking of the campus of a girls school that was named after her, campus ChoMeSh (acronym for Chaya Mushka Shneersohn).

The importance of commemorating his wife's legacy through positive actions and initiatives became evident from the Rebbe's words spoken after the *shivah*, when he tearfully thanked the thousands who had come to console him, saying:

> "Each of those who consoled and blessed me should see blessings [in their own lives] literally with their own eyes…additional gratitude and blessings to those who initiated projects [in her honor]…."[61]

In response to a woman who wanted to commemorate a loved one and was unsure if she should commission a Torah scroll or an Ark for a synagogue, the Rebbe recommended a different kind of memorial[62]:

There is a third option, which has precedence over the other two, and that is to "adopt" a yeshiva student who is learning our eternal Torah, i.e., sponsor a student in the yeshiva, where he or she can learn our holy Torah.[63]

The Rebbe's approach to honoring those who died was to do something to benefit the living—to create the kind of commemoration that would bring more goodness into the world, thus spiritually "nourishing" the souls of the departed as well.

On February 29, 1960, a 5.7-magnitude earthquake devastated the city of Agadir, Morocco, killing 12,000 people (about a third of the city's population at the time), including some students of the local Chabad yeshiva. The Rebbe immediately dispatched a telegram to Rabbi Shaul Danan, the Chief Rabbi of Agadir, expressing solidarity:

> Together with our dear Moroccan brethren, we bemoan the "fire that ravaged" the community of Agadir, and our heartfelt prayers are with you.... May G-d bless you in your efforts of rebuilding with inner peace and magnanimity....
>
> P.S. I have encouraged the Chabad community to increase their prayers and charity this Thursday, which is a fast day, in commemoration of the tragedy.[64]

At the Purim *farbrengen* the following week, the Rebbe spoke publicly about the disaster in Agadir. He talked about the idea that the restoration after destruction could be even more powerful than what was there prior to the destruction. He brought the example of the second tablets at Mount Sinai, which contained many additions and were "double in strength" in comparison to the first set. And he said:

> Therefore, in the place of one [learning] center, there must be numerous ones, and in the place of one student there must be many more…! This growth will not only benefit the community and school but also the souls of the departed, who were sadly cut down in their prime, and who will derive gratification when the empty places on the yeshiva benches they left behind will once again be filled.[65]

It is only natural to want some tangible way to hold on to the memory of our departed loved ones. The Rebbe taught us that the best way to do this is not just by creating memorials of bricks and stone but by pursuing positive deeds that will benefit the departed souls, as well as create a tangible benefit for the living.

CHAPTER 11

APPRECIATING LIFE'S GIFTS AND OPPORTUNITIES

In addition to seeing the time after a loved one's passing as an occasion to engage in positive action on behalf of the deceased, the Rebbe saw it as a time for a more introspective kind of activity. It is a time when those who are left in this world are more conscious of their own soul and therefore have the capacity to examine anew the spiritual and emotional quality of their lives.

In a letter written to Rabbi Herbert Weiner, noted author of *Nine and a Half Mystics*, after the rabbi's mother passed away, the Rebbe writes:

The above provides an insight into what seems to be a somewhat "incongruous" observation by Maimonides,[66] namely, that the period of mourning observed by a bereaved family has to do with *teshuvah* [repentance].... For this is a fitting time to reflect upon the opportunities that have been given to the soul to "return" to its Source while it is here on earth, housed in its body, and, in this experience of *teshuvah*, to live a meaningful and happy life to a ripe old age.[67]

When we reflect on the loss of a loved one and the way his or her soul returned to its Source, we become more open to the needs of our own soul and to developing its relationship with G-d while there is still time to do so in this world.

The importance of utilizing the unique and passing opportunities afforded us during our physical stay on earth can be seen from the following story.

In 1941, the sixth Lubavitcher Rebbe, Rabbi Yosef Yitzchak Schneersohn, instituted a program that provided Jewish children from New York City public schools with an hour of weekly Jewish study.

Every Wednesday afternoon, student volunteers from the Lubavitch yeshiva would interrupt their studies for several hours, travel to New York City's public schools, bring their charges to local synagogues, and teach them about their traditions, then escort them back to their respective schools.

One studious young man wrote to the Rebbe, asking to be excused from participating in the program, as he felt he was wasting his time.

First, he wrote, he didn't think that he actually achieved very much. Every week he recited prayers with the children but didn't believe that the prayer sessions had any lasting effect.

Second, it took three or four hours out of his day to travel to the school assigned to him, pick up the children, teach them, and drop them off, then return to the yeshiva. He felt that his time would be better spent furthering his studies.

The Rebbe replied: "I want you to know that on Wednesday afternoons, all of the souls in *Gan Eden*, including Moses himself, envy you for the unique opportunity you have each week to say *Shema Yisrael* and recite a blessing with a Jewish child. Their souls no longer have the opportunity to interact with Jewish children and bring them closer to their Father in Heaven. Do you know what they would give for the privilege that you have?"[68]

This story brings to life the monumental teaching of the Mishnah,[69] which states, that "One hour of good deeds in this world is more desirable than the entire World to Come." Reflecting on our mortality and that the spiritual opportunities, or *mitzvot*, we encounter during our lifetime are bound up with physical existence helps to heighten the sense of significance and urgency surrounding these unique opportunities, which, in turn, inspires us to positive action.

As the following anecdote demonstrates, the sensitive time after a death also grants us clarity of perspective, making it an appropriate time to express gratitude for the abundant blessings that grace our lives and for the loving relationships we still have.

The Rebbe was separated from his parents in the 1920s, when he was twenty-six years old, and did not reunite with his mother until 1947. His father had passed away three years earlier. The Rebbe often expressed his anguish at not having had the opportunity to fulfill his obligation of honoring his parents for so many years.

When the Rebbe first met his mother after all their years of separation, they embraced for twenty minutes without uttering a word. After this reunion, he visited her every day, walking to her house in the late afternoon to serve her tea and converse.

Soon after his mother died in 1965, the Rebbe was visited by a teenage girl who wanted to discuss a conflict she was having with her mother. She was angry that her mother would not give her as much allowance money as she felt she needed. The Rebbe replied with sadness: "I just lost my mother this year. Do you know how much money I would give to see her just once more?"[70]

In this instance, the Rebbe utilized his own sense of personal loss and grief over the loss of his mother to help strengthen the bonds of another family. Reflecting on the transience of life can help us better appreciate and cherish the loving relationships we are blessed to have but often take for granted.

CHAPTER 12

CONSOLATION THROUGH ACTIVITY

An important theme in the Rebbe's teachings is that intensified activity after a loss helps foster a heightened sense of purpose and can be an important means of achieving comfort.

In 1956, after a vicious terrorist attack at a school in the Israeli town of Kfar Chabad had claimed six lives (see chapter 14 for more on this story), the local inhabitants were completely devastated and found themselves despondent.

In the words of a newspaper article that appeared at the time, "Despair and dejection pervaded the village and began to eat away at its foundations. Some officials in town wanted to close the school down. Others saw what happened as a sign that their dream of a peaceful life in the Holy Land was premature. Perhaps we should disband, seek refuge in safer havens? The village was slowly dying."

The Rebbe's reaction? While Judaism does not provide explanations for tragedy, it does have a response. Thus the Rebbe's message to the stricken village was: Do not diminish or detract from your noble activities, but increase and expand them![71]

The doubts the residents of Kfar Chabad had begun to harbor regarding their communal project of establishing a town were exacerbated by their preoccupation with grave thoughts and pessimistic conversations. Only by immersing themselves in activities of further growth would they begin to see their mission in a better light, and their faith in its future would blossom again.

In his response to the people of Kfar Chabad, the Rebbe wasn't making light of the very real security issue that existed. In fact, very soon after the tragedy occurred, he contacted Mr. Zalman Shazar, the future president of Israel, to discuss issues of security. But, at the outset, the Rebbe focused on providing moral support and encouragement. His message was clear: Consolation is achieved through intensified activity, a heightened sense of purpose, and by redirecting our thoughts from what has been lost to that which thankfully remains.[72]

A moving teaching of Rabbi Chaim Ibn Attar,

known as the *Or HaChaim*,[73] about the mourning of Jacob for his son Joseph, elucidates this point:

In the book of Genesis, we read of the heart-wrenching story of Joseph and his brothers. Jacob, convinced that his beloved son Joseph had been devoured by wild beasts, is overcome by sorrow. The Torah relates that Jacob rent his garments, placed sackcloth on his loins, and said, "I will go down to my grave mourning for my son." He refused to be comforted, but his family didn't stop trying. Indeed, "All his sons and all his daughters arose to comfort him...."[74]

The *Or HaChaim* observes that Jacob's children didn't utter a word of consolation. The situation was beyond words, since Jacob had declared himself inconsolable. But they gathered, all eleven sons, daughters, and throngs of grandchildren, and "arose" in order "to comfort him." They knew that nothing they could say or do would make good the past. But what they could do was simply present themselves to him, shining the spotlight on Jacob's large and beautiful family, highlighting the blessed present and its promising growth into the future.

Immediately following this account, the Torah delivers another lesson on the effect of intensified activity after a trauma.

Judah had tragically lost two of his sons. Not long afterward, he lost his wife as well. How does a man who loses everything find comfort? "He went up to oversee his sheepshearers."[75] He threw himself into developing his business affairs. By focusing on a project and putting his mind and heart into it, he was helping his wounds to heal.

The Rebbe made a similar point to a grieving widow who had tragically lost two daughters to illness. A short while after completing the *shivah* for her second daughter, she wrote a heartbreaking letter to the Rebbe asking how G-d could take two of her children after taking her husband. She concluded her letter by asking how she could go on living with such pain.

To her last question, the Rebbe responded that the way to conquer her pain would be "through devoting herself to easing (literally sweetening) the lives of 'the widower and orphans,'" meaning her son-in-law and grandchildren. This, the Rebbe wrote, would be a channel for her grief and help her attain some degree of solace and comfort.[76]

The Rebbe conveyed a similar message to Rabbi Raphael Grossman and his wife when they came to seek his guidance and comfort after the sudden, devastating passing of their seventeen-year-old daughter. After advising them on a life-changing course of action they were contemplating, the Rebbe said gently: "And as far as lasting consolation is concerned, you will achieve true comfort through the positive accomplishments you attain going forward, especially those related to honoring and immortalizing the memory of your precious daughter, of blessed memory."[77]

In the same vein, when Rabbi Mordechai and Freida Sufrin were grieving after their newborn had passed away, the Rebbe gently suggested: "It would be advisable to make every effort to have another child."

CHAPTER 13

THINK GOOD

When catastrophe strikes, the mind can become prone to fearful imaginings, especially when there have been repeated disasters. People in these situations often live in fear of what will happen next, replaying possible scenarios in their minds: "Will it happen again? Will calamity reoccur, at the same time, same place, in the same way, or worse?"

Aside from the obvious inner turmoil wreaked by such terrifying thoughts, Judaism teaches that our negative thoughts can actually affect reality for the worse, often becoming self-fulfilling prophecies.

This message can be discerned in the biblical account of Joseph's dream interpretations during his incarceration in an Egyptian prison:[78]

At that time, Pharaoh's chief butler and chief baker fell from grace and were placed behind bars, where they confided their dreams to Joseph. The butler dreamed that "Pharaoh's cup was in my hand and I took the grapes, pressed them into the cup, and placed it on Pharaoh's palm." The baker dreamed that "birds were eating from the baskets [of bread] on my head"—something birds would be afraid to do from a living human.[79]

Joseph interpreted these dreams to mean that the butler would be restored to his position by Pharaoh, while the baker would be hanged and his flesh picked off of him by the ravenous birds of his nightmare. A few days later, these predictions indeed came to pass. While we can read this as an incident of prophetic dreaming and skilled dream analysis, the story can also be read as an insight into how our inner thoughts have power over our destinies. In keeping with the Talmud's observation that nocturnal dreams merely echo daydreams and conscious thoughts, the butler was clearly optimistic about his fate, while the baker thought in more morbid terms.

A distressed rabbi once wrote to the Rebbe that his synagogue had recently received a new Torah scroll whose kosher status had been brought into question twice. He was very concerned, because within a correspondingly short period of time, two young members of his community had passed away, and he worried that there was a correlation between the unfortunate events.

The Rebbe responded by quoting a famous teaching of the third Lubavitcher Rebbe, the Tzemach Tzedek:

Tracht gut vet zein gut, "Think good, and it will be good." That is, the mere exercise of thinking positively produces positive results.[80] In case the teaching would be taken glibly or be seen as a platitude, the Rebbe then made reference to a Talmudic text.

The Talmudic passage he cited[81] discusses dreams and their interpretations, including an episode where on many occasions Raba sought out the interpretation skills of a certain Bar Hedya. The dream-readings were mainly negative and yielded tragic results, among them the death of Raba's wife and some of his children. The Talmud continues:

> Bar Hedya was once traveling with Raba in a boat. As he was disembarking, he let fall a book. Raba found it and saw written in it: "All dreams follow the mouth." He exclaimed: "Wretch! It all depended on you, and you gave me all this pain!"[82]

According to a related Talmudic discussion, the same principle applies to daytime thoughts as well:

> It once happened that Hillel the Elder was returning from a journey, and he heard a great cry in the city, and he said: "I am confident that this does not come from my house." Of him Scripture says: "He shall not be afraid of evil tidings; his heart is steadfast, trusting in the Lord (Psalms 112:7).

Raba said: "Whenever you expound this verse, you may make the second clause explain the first, or the first clause explain the second. You may make the second clause explain the first, thus: 'He will not fear evil tidings.' Why? Because 'his heart is steadfast, trusting in the Lord.' You may explain the second clause by the first, thus: 'His heart is steadfast, trusting in the Lord,' and therefore, 'he shall not be afraid of evil things.'"[83]

The Talmud then relates another story:

Once Rabbi Judah ben Natan sighed, and Rabbi Hamnuna said to him: "This man wants to bring suffering on himself, since it is written (in Job 3:25), 'For one thing that I fear has befallen me, and what I dreaded has overtaken me.'"[84]

In an address the Rebbe gave in 1963,[85] he expanded on the philosophical and spiritual dynamic behind the principle "Think good, and it will be good."

He began by asking the obvious question: On the basis of what should one believe that in the face of any challenge, "it (the outcome) will be good"? Isn't it presumptuous to assume that in every given situation we are always deserving of Divine grace, regardless of our state of religious and moral standing[86]?

And what of the basic Jewish belief that there is a Divine order of reward and punishment[87] that governs our world, making salvation dependent on righteous behavior?

The Rebbe's answer was: When a Jew decides to place his trust in G-d, believing that his current crisis will be resolved favorably despite facing a bleak reality that suggests otherwise, he has, in effect, risen above his own nature, which in turn elicits, reciprocally, "measure for measure" the suspension of the Divine order,[88] where only the righteous are deserving of salvation.

G-d, the creator of Man, understands how difficult and even "supernatural" it is for a human being to truly believe—*to the degree that he or she no longer experiences fear and anxiety*—that an unpromising and even seemingly hopeless situation will have a positive outcome. And, thus, as a result and even *reward* for the extraordinary act of worship of *"tracht gut,"* G-d deems the believer, who is otherwise undeserving of a positive outcome, to be deserving in this instance of an extra measure of Divine generosity.

What follows are a small sampling of the hundreds of letters the Rebbe wrote in which he referred to the aphorism, *"tracht gut vet zein gut."*[89]

In response to an individual who sent the Rebbe a telegram seeking his blessing for good health, the Rebbe wrote:

I received your telegram stating that your operation will be taking place on Sunday…and certainly everything will work out and return to normal.

I have already written [in the past] expressing my astonishment with those who look to interpret events that occur to them or members of their family in a "strict" [i.e., negative, even morbid] manner, even though my father-in-law, the [previous] Rebbe, has stated numerous times in the name of his predecessors the teaching: "Think positive, and [the outcome] will be positive," and certainly [this is meant literally, that] *things will be good*!

…I look forward to being informed in the future of the fact that things have turned out well and your situation has improved.

Awaiting good news and with blessings to you and yours.[90]

In his response to an individual who had requested that the Rebbe pray for his wife and granddaughter, who were both unwell, the Rebbe elaborated on this theme:

In response to your two letters [requesting blessings for the good health of] your wife and granddaughter…Divine mercy will definitely be aroused for them so that they return to good health.

…I strongly discourage the behavior of those

who dwell on, exaggerate, and amplify their health issues through speaking about and writing about any and every health issue they encounter, which runs contrary to the philosophy of the Rabbeim who taught, "Think positive, and the outcome will be positive."

If this is the case with regards to positive *thought* [which can affect reality for the better], how much more so when it comes to positive speech and writing, which is considered to be like deed.[91]

In the following response to someone who, it seems, had written several pessimistic letters to the Rebbe describing his life's challenges, the Rebbe elaborated on the effects of verbalizing negative thoughts.

In his letter, the Rebbe highlights the novelty of the teaching, "*Think* good, etc.," which teaches that the process of actualization, where a spiritual idea and energy becomes manifest in physical reality, does not begin through verbalizing an idea (a common point made in Chasidic texts) but begins earlier, and on a more spiritual plane, through the process of thought.

In response to your letter, from which it is clear that I have not yet been successful at inspiring in you a spirit of optimism, despite having told you on numerous occasions that according to Jewish teaching, one should refrain from [verbally] introducing negative and melancholy ideas into the world, which is one way to help avert the actualization of negativity.[92]

And not only does this apply to *verbalization*—which, according to Chasidic teaching[93], contains the power to actualize, as we learn from the behavior of the Maggid [of Mezritch], who would verbalize his novel ideas in order to "bring them into the world"—but even *thought* has the power to effect actualization, as we see from the teaching of our Rabbeim, "*Think* good, and it *will be good*," which is why one should refrain from negative thinking, so as not actualize negativity.[94]

In a different letter, the Rebbe responded strongly to a yeshiva student, who wrote to the Rebbe in the middle of summer about his plans to return home from his yeshiva during the High Holy Days to be with his father, who wasn't well at the time. After blessing the student's father with good health, the Rebbe wrote:

> P.S. Regarding the idea you proposed in your letter, to be at home over the High Holy Days, even though many students will be at the yeshiva, since your father is currently unwell: I was greatly surprised and taken aback by the apparent lack of trust in G-d, which allows you to assume and make concrete plans (to leave the spiritual environment of yeshiva and, as a result, decrease in your dedication to heartfelt prayer[95]) as a result,

already now *in the middle of the summer* that your father will still be unwell in a month's time!

It would be far better and more advisable to assume instead, per the dictate of the Rabbeim, "Think positive, and the outcome will be positive," that your father's health will definitely have improved by then, allowing you to devote greater energies to your spiritual development."[96]

The previous letter brings to mind the following story:

During a private audience with the Rebbe, a chasid mentioned that he was due to have a very serious operation in a few weeks' time, and he asked the Rebbe for a blessing that the surgery be a success. The Rebbe grew very serious and said pointedly, "Instead of asking that I pray that the surgery be successful, you could have asked me to pray that you not need to undergo surgery at all!"[97]

This story teaches that not only do our actual thoughts affect reality, but even our attitude and *way of thinking* (which reflects our degree of faith) profoundly impacts our reality for better or worse.

In addition to the negative effects of pessimistic thinking on reality, the Rebbe strongly discouraged negative thinking and visualization because of its depressing and despair-inducing psychological effects, which can lead to physiological deterioration as well.

Consider the following candid letter of the Rebbe, written to an individual who wasn't satisfied with the medical advice given him by his doctors and decided to research his condition by reading some medical books and journals and draw his own conclusions.

> In response to your letter in which you inform me of the numerous operations you underwent in the past, etc.
>
> …It is unfortunate that you have set out to research and read up on the medical condition you assume to be your own. In my opinion, you should concern yourself instead, per the Torah's directives, with following the doctors' orders and to engage your mind and heart, and all of your powers of concentration, with thoughts of trust in G-d, the Healer of all who are sick, who can create wonders.
>
> It is surely not advisable to mix into the medical research [of your condition], which is not your domain [but that of your doctors], especially if this disturbs your inner peace and triggers thoughts of depression and despair. [On this note] the teaching of the Rebbes of Chabad, "Think positive, and the outcome will be positive," is well known.[98]

The Rebbe elaborated on this theme in the following letter he wrote in 1952 to a woman who was ill:

> While I am pleased to read in your letter the quotation about G-d being the Creator of the world, Who also guides all its destinies, etc., this very good impression is weakened by the further tone of your letter, where you state that you want to be "realistic," based on the prognosis of physicians regarding your condition. I want to tell you, first, that even from the realistic point of view, we must recognize the fact that very many times, the greatest physicians have made mistakes in diagnosis. Moreover, in recent times we see that new discoveries are made daily in the medical field, with new "wonder" drugs and methods, which have revolutionized medical treatment.
>
> Secondly, observing life in general, we see so many things that are strange and unbelievable that to be truly realistic, one cannot consider anything as impossible.[99]
>
> In a condition that is, to a large extent, bound up with the nervous system and the resistance of the organism, even medical opinion agrees that the stronger the patient's faith in cure, and the stronger his will to get better, the stronger becomes his ability to recover. Needless to say, this is not said in the way of an admonition. But, inasmuch as by individual Divine Providence, you have learned of me, and I of you, I think I

am entitled to convey to you the above thoughts, which I was privileged to hear from my father-in-law, of saintly memory, in similar cases.

May the Almighty help you to fulfill your promise to work for Torah-true movements and to bring up your children in the way of true Yiddishkeit.[100]

The connection between one's emotional and physical state of being was an important feature[101] of the Rebbe's thinking and can be seen from the care he took never to use the common Hebrew word for hospital, *beit cholim*, which literally means "house of the sick," clearly a very discouraging way to refer to the very institution that is meant to inspire confidence and hope.

In a letter to Professor Mordechai Shani, director of the Sheba medical center at Tel Hashomer in Israel, the Rebbe made reference to an earlier conversation they had had in which he had strongly urged him to call the hospital a *beit refuah* (house of healing) instead of *beit cholim*. "Even though…this would seem to represent a semantic change, the term *beit refuah* brings encouragement to the sick…."[102]

The same concern led the Rebbe to caution doctors in the way they discuss medical issues with their patients.

"Surely you are aware of the comment of many of our great Rebbes on the ruling of the Sages—'He [the doctor] shall provide for his cure.' From these words, we derive that physicians have been granted permission to heal"—that the only mandate that doctors have been granted is *to heal* [and not to induce despair]."[103]

The following related story demonstrates the Rebbe's insistence that the physician's domain is diagnosis, not prognosis.

After his wife had been diagnosed with a life-threatening illness, a distraught husband came to see the Rebbe, bringing along his two little children.

"Rebbe," he broke down crying, "I am a man who just immigrated to the United States with my family. I can't even speak English! And now my wife is going to die, leaving me to care for these two little children!"

"Who said she will die?" the Rebbe asked, visibly upset. "The doctor," he responded. "Do you have the prognosis with you?" the Rebbe asked.

"Yes," said the man, handing it to the Rebbe. The Rebbe took the paper and tore it up. "Since when do doctors determine who will live and who will die?" he demanded. "Only G-d can do that! Now, go home and tell your wife that she should continue taking her prescribed medication, and she will be fine."

Happily, this woman, a wife and mother, lived for many years.[104]

PART II

HELPING OTHERS COPE WITH LOSS

CHAPTER 14

SILENCE

On the night of April 11, 1956, a band of Palestinian terrorists entered the Israeli village of Kfar Chabad. They made their way to the synagogue of the local agricultural school, where the school's young students were in the midst of the evening prayers, and raked the room with fire from their Karl-Gustav rifles. They reaped a cruel blood-harvest: five children and one teacher were killed and another ten children wounded, their pure blood soaking the prayerbooks that fell from their hands and splattering the synagogue's white-washed walls.

The residents of the village, many of whom had escaped the horrors of the Nazi Holocaust and the Stalinist years of terror, were shattered. A large number of the students' parents traveled to Kfar Chabad to take their children home, to the point that the administrators of the school were considering to shut it down entirely. Some proposed that the fledgling village be disbanded—that it was simply too dangerous to live there.

Despair and dejection pervaded the village and began to eat away at its foundations.

The Rebbe's responses, which came in the form of a telegram sent upon the close of the *shivah* (week of mourning) and numerous follow-up letters, infused life, vitality, and hope into the village. The prevalent theme of the Rebbe's communications was: Your response to the murders must be to continue to build, to continue to expand your educational activities, to continue to grow both materially and spiritually. This will be your response to the evil of the terrorists, and in this you will find consolation and strength. The Rebbe also dispatched a delegation of twelve rabbinical students, as his personal representatives, to spend time in Kfar Chabad and visit other communities throughout Israel and convey his message of encouragement.

There were two striking things about the Rebbe's response. The first was his delay in communicating to the stricken village. Many wondered: Why did the Rebbe wait a full week before sending his message of encouragement?

In addition, many expected the Rebbe to offer some sort of theological "explanation" for the tragedy. This he steadfastly refused to do. All inquiries along the line of "why did this happen?" were met with silence.

The Rebbe himself explained his behavior in a number of letters, as well as in a public talk he delivered a few weeks after the incident.[105]

In one letter, the Rebbe wrote:

> It appears from your letter that you are wondering why I did not write immediately following the event. Yet the Torah attests regarding Aaron the High Priest that "he was silent." Certainly, and how much more so, should it be so in our case.[106]

The Rebbe is referring to the episode, related in the 10 chapter of the Book of Leviticus, where Aaron's two sons tragically died on the day of the Sanctuary's inaugurations. The Torah related that "Aaron was silent," indicating that at the moment of tragedy, the only appropriate response is silence.

In another letter, this one in response to someone who proposed a theological explanation for the tragedy, the Rebbe again cited Aaron's silence as the appropriate model to emulate. The Rebbe was quick to add, however:

> The above applies only regarding any attempt to *explain* the tragedy. But as far as the *outcome* necessitated by the tragedy is concerned, our response is clear. Beginning with the experience of

our forefathers in Egypt thousands of years ago, every affliction in Jewish history has its response explicitly spelled out (Exodus 1:12): "As much as they afflicted them, so much did they increase, and so much were they strengthened."[107]

The Rebbe's behavior in this incident serves as a key lesson in responding to news of tragedy.

The most helpful thing we can do for those who suffer loss, particularly in the first hours and days, is to simply be there for them. We may have words of wisdom to share, but that is not what the mourners need from us at this moment. They not yet ready for the pain of loss to be mitigated, and to attempt to do so can in fact be experienced as an affront to their loss. Rather, what they need from us at this point is simply for us to share in their sorrow.

As Maimonides writes in his code of Jewish law, "We do not relate teachings of Torah law or homiletic insights in the home of a mourner. Instead, we sit in grief." Maimonides also rules that those who come to visit the mourner "are not permitted to say anything until the mourner speaks first."[108]

I remember hearing a therapist lecture on the topic of how to deal with others' losses. He related that he once traveled for four hours to visit a friend in mourning. The entire way he was thinking of something to say. How could he bring comfort to his friend who was in such pain? When he got there he still hadn't come up with anything wise, so he decided to say nothing. After sitting in silence for a while, he said the prescribed prayer of condolence and left for home. Half a year later, he met up with his friend, who told him: "I want you to know that your condolence call made such a difference to me. I was so touched that you traveled all the way to my home without saying a thing to me. You obviously came simply to be with me and share in my pain, and that was very comforting."

CHAPTER 15

EMPATHY

There are different types of silence. There is the silence that comes from a lack of words. There is a silence that comes from holding back what shouldn't be said. And then there is a silence of connection, of identification. And that is a silence that speaks louder than any words can. It is created not by unspoken syllables and sounds but by palpable feelings communicated through presence. The comfort that we can offer through this kind of empathic silence transcends the spoken word, coming straight from the heart.

Yehudah Avner was an Israeli diplomat who as a seventeen-year-old boy fought in Israel's War of Independence. During the siege of Jerusalem, Avner lost two of his friends—including a girl named Esther, the sister of the woman who would later become his wife. In a private audience, Avner related this part of his life story to the Rebbe. This is how he describes the Rebbe's response:

I always found that responses from the Rebbe were not always in words. There was a look; it could be a mesmerizing look. Anybody who has ever met the Lubavitcher Rebbe will always remember those eyes. And also there was…a certain nod…. On that occasion, he didn't respond with words but…there was a vibrancy of understanding and compassion when I told him about the death of my wife's sister.[109]

A similar account was shared by a woman named Marguerite Kozenn-Chajes, who had been a successful opera singer in Vienna in the late 1930s and performed in front of Hitler, may his name be erased, at the Salzburger Festspiele in August 1939. On the night of her performance at the festival, Marguerite was smuggled out of Austria by her friends, and she managed to embark on the last boat to the US before the war broke out just a few days later. She later settled with her family in Detroit, where she became founder and president of the Pro Mozart Society of Greater Detroit.

Years later Marguerite's daughter grew up and married a doctor who, in 1959, was honored at the dinner of a Chabad institution. In conjunction with that occasion, Marguerite had an audience with the Rebbe.

"I walked into the Rebbe's room," Marguerite related, "I cannot explain why, but suddenly, for the first time since the Holocaust, I felt that I could cry. I, like so many other survivors who had lost entire families, never cried before. We knew that if we would start crying, we might never stop, and that in order to survive, we could not express our emotions. But at that moment, it was as though the dam obstructing my inner waterfall of tears was removed. I began sobbing like a baby. I shared with the Rebbe my entire story: My innocent childhood, becoming a star in Vienna, performing in front of Hitler, escaping to the US, and learning of the death of my closest kin.

"The Rebbe listened. But he not only listened with his ears. He listened with his eyes, with his heart, with his soul, and he took it all in. I shared all of my experiences, and he absorbed it all. That night, I felt like I was given a second father. I felt that the Rebbe adopted me as his daughter."[110]

When we interact with people who have experienced loss, our natural response is often to try to ease their pain. But, in fact, the best way to do that is to be present in a way that allows the bereaved to express their sorrow.

My uncle, who tragically lost a young child, later wrote that many people who came to the house of mourning to make a *shivah* call tried to divert his attention from his grief. But he did not want to be diverted. He wanted to talk about his beloved son and share his loss with his visitors. He wanted to feel that they missed his child too. "Only such company can lessen sorrow," he wrote. "But if people talk of other things, good as their intentions may be, the pain remains as deep as it was before they came."[111]

By being open with our own emotions, by freely shedding tears alongside the mourner, we help the bereaved express their hurt so that it can be dealt with, and over time, healed.

There are numerous accounts of Holocaust survivors who came to the Rebbe seeking counsel and solace. To their surprise, instead of trying to rationalize the past or bolster them with an encouraging message, the Rebbe would gently ask them about their families. How many loved ones did they lose, what were their names, and what were they like....

The survivors would inevitably break down in tears, as would the Rebbe.

Indeed, while the Rebbe generally exhibited little emotion in public, when it came to human tragedy, he would often choke up or weep openly and profusely in middle of addressing thousands of his Chasidim. He did not try to bottle up his own grief, thus providing a powerful lesson in how to respond to the painful events in our personal lives and in our communities.

CHAPTER 16

SENSITIVITY

True empathy requires us to put ourselves in others' shoes. Thus the question we should ask ourselves when responding to tragedy is not, "What would I want others to do for me were I, G-d forbid, in a similar situation?" but, "What would the bereaved want from those seeking to help ease their pain?"

This type of reflection could help avert misplaced efforts or offers to honor the departed, which can bring unnecessary pain to the family, especially if these offers are perceived as a veiled attempt to take advantage of the situation in order to advance someone's agenda.

The Rebbe's sensitivity to this issue can be seen in the postscript to the aforementioned letter[112] he wrote to Rabbi Herbert Weiner after the loss of the rabbi's mother:

> P.S. On the basis of our personal acquaintance and what I have heard about you from mutual friends, I take the liberty of suggesting to you

that in addition to [reciting] *Kaddish* in the daily prayers, as is customary, you should also study a practical Jewish law publicly, such as from the *Kitzur Shulchan Aruch* (Code of Jewish Law). This is of special importance in our day and age, and it has many worthwhile implications. Above all, it is a *zechut horabim* ("public merit"), coupled with a special *zechut* for the soul of the departed. Also, furthering adherence to the Will of G-d, especially by a person of influence, gives practical expression to [the opening words of the *Kaddish*] "Glorified and sanctified be G-d's name...."[113]

Following this, the Rebbe added:

This entire piece has been written as a P.S. and on a separate sheet not because it is of lesser importance than the letter preceding it. However, our Sages wisely reminded us that allowances should be made for a person in distress. The thought might just occur that here comes a man who is not a relative and wishes to take "advantage" of a profound and unhappy experience in order to advance "his ideals." For this reason, this part of the letter has been separated from the first.

Surely, no one felt as strongly about the ideal of promoting Jewish practice than the Rebbe did, and yet, that ideal, however noble, was superseded by his sensitivity to the needs of the bereaved.

CHAPTER 17

EXPLAINING DEATH TO CHILDREN

On the day of Yom Kippur in 1973, Israel was suddenly attacked by Egypt, and in the ensuing battle with Egyptian forces, many lives were lost. Following the war, the Rebbe sent letters of encouragement to the wounded and to the families of those who lost their lives.

One of those who sought advice from the Rebbe was a widow who struggled to explain death to her young, orphaned children. She wrote:

> To the esteemed Rabbi Menachem Mendel Schneerson, may you live and be well....
>
> During this very difficult time [of war], G-d was with us, and we succeeded in standing strong against all of the nations. Nevertheless...because I remain a widow with no father for my children, it is hard for me to educate them and to bring them up in the best and proper way. It is hard for me to stand alone against such a large world with all the adversity out there. Because my children have

a proud Jewish heritage, Rebbe, I have questions that I would like to ask.

I have one daughter who is seven years old and one boy who is five. How do I explain that their father's death came through self-sacrifice to G-d's will?

My son is asking me, "Mother, when Moshiach comes, the dead will return and then Father will come back. So why doesn't Moshiach come now?"

How do I answer these questions? In my eyes, these questions, which are so fundamental, may have an effect on my children's beliefs and thoughts.

I would be honored if the Rebbe would advise me.

The Rebbe answered:

Explain to [your children] the way it is in truth: that there are souls that are so pure and holy that G-d wants them to be in the heavens, after they have completed their mission in this world, and guard over all the sons and daughters of Israel who live in the Holy Land.[114]

Orphaned children are often plagued by doubts about their parent's early passing. They might wonder if a premature death is a sign of deficiency, or even iniquity, in their parent. These kinds of speculations can lead children to develop feelings of shame around the memory of their parent and his or her death.

In his response, the Rebbe addresses this issue in

a twofold manner. First, he explains that, in general, untimely death can be a sign of remarkable virtue, of "a soul so pure and holy that G-d wants them to be in heaven" or of one who was quick to "complete their mission in this world." Second, the Rebbe points out that, in the case of their father, the noble mission was clear to all; he had altruistically sacrificed his life to "guard over all of the sons and daughters of Israel." Is there a greater merit in the world?

There's another insightful detail to be learned from the Rebbe's words: "Explain to them *the way it is in truth*...." Perhaps with these few words, he was subtly telling the widow that this is not just a sugarcoated way of explaining death to children, but it is the true reality—and a belief which, if she could make it her own, would be transmitted to her children too.

The Rebbe's letter characteristically concludes by emphasizing the possibility for a continued positive relationship between the father and the children:

> In the heavens, [those who were taken] intercede for all their relatives and loved ones, and especially for their children, and they ask from G-d that their children succeed in their studies and conduct. When their children conduct themselves properly, that is the biggest pleasure that the soul can have—and that's how it continues to remain alive.

PART III

RESPONSES TO SOCIETAL AND GLOBAL TRAGEDIES

CHAPTER 18

THE JEWISH ANSWER TO EVIL

When tragedy occurs on a community level, the shock and sense of vulnerability can be paralyzing. Difficult questions are raised, such as "What do we do now? Should we fold up or scale back on our efforts and presence? Is this a sign that we're in the wrong place, that this will never work?"

In chapter 12 above, we quoted the Rebbe's response to the stricken residents of Kfar Chabad after their village was attacked by terrorists:

> While Judaism does not provide explanations for tragedy, it does have a response. Do not diminish or detract from your noble activities but increase and expand them!

Consolation can be achieved through intensified activity, a heightened sense of purpose, and by redirecting our thoughts from what has been lost to that which thankfully remains.

By choosing to rebuild and intensify growth in the face of loss—and especially in the face of terrorism and acts of hatred—we also make a statement of victory. We become living proof that evil does not prevail, that life triumphs over death. Conversely, reducing positive efforts and activities only contributes to promoting the ideological goals of evildoers.

An ancient iteration of this argument can be found in Midrashic lore,[115] as articulated by Miriam the prophetess when she was a child. After Pharaoh had decreed that all newborn Hebrew males be thrown into the Nile, Miriam's parents, Amram and Yocheved, who held leadership positions among the children of Israel, divorced, leading other Israelites to divorce as well. Miriam went to her father and challenged him, saying, "Pharaoh decreed against the males, but you have passed a decree against the females as well."

As a result of this argument, which brought about Yocheved and Amram's reunion, none other than Moses, Pharaoh's nemesis, was born. And it was this argument that was responsible for the high Jewish birth rate despite the slavery in Egypt.

Miriam's argument was certainly not intuitive, and

the counterargument would echo throughout much of Jewish history including, most recently, the Holocaust: "Who in their right mind could bring children into such a dark and turbulent world?" During the time of the first Jewish holocaust in Egypt—when newborn infants were being used for spare building parts, and a campaign of genocide was being waged against male infants—having children must have seemed, at the very least, irresponsible. And, yet, as Miriam argued, the Jewish people believed that by not having children, they would only be contributing to the program of extermination their enemies planned for them.

In a frank letter he wrote to Eli Wiesel (the Holocaust survivor whose activism and writings won him the Noble Peace Prize), the Rebbe advocated a similar approach to those who had recently undergone the trauma and devastation of the Holocaust:

> And now allow me to make a personal observation which is related to our discussion when you visited me last. Your article series titled, "And the world was silent," reawakened in me the idea I'd like to communicate here.
>
> To remember and not forget, as the Torah teaches, "Do not forget that which Amalek did to you…"[116] is obviously an active thing, in the language of the rabbis, a "positive command."

That notwithstanding, remembering alone is only one aspect of our responsibility. The other, and arguably more important, aspect is the active combat against the so-called "final solution" that Hitler, may his name be obliterated, like Haman in his day, had in mind to do.

This combat should express itself through deeds that recall the Jewish response to infanticide in Egypt, "they would increase, and they would multiply."

To achieve this aim, it doesn't help to only feel sad and constantly remind oneself of the horrific tragedies that once were and of the importance not to forget. Rather, we must expand and publicize the efforts to grow the Jewish people literally, and in the spirit of "they would increase, and they would multiply"—in contradiction to the "final solution."

In this matter, as in all matters, the important thing is to provide a living example, especially someone like yourself who underwent the horrors that you did, who will demonstrate that Hitler did not prevail. Even if only in order to spite him, one should have a large family of children and grandchildren.

With all the conviction I can muster, I'd like to say that notwithstanding the importance of telling the younger generation about the tragic experiences and losses suffered and how difficult it is to be liberated from those terrifying memories and ordeals of the past, in my estimation, the main calling of our times is to fulfill the teaching which states, "Against your will, you must live,"[117] with the emphasis on "you must live"…i.e., you must make the effort to establish a Jewish home and family, which will certainly contribute to the downfall of Hitler, proving futile his efforts that there be one chasid of Vizhnitz less….[118]

At the conclusion of this long letter (only a portion of which is quoted here), the Rebbe ends:

Too long a letter? If, however, with good fortune you will be married after the festival of Shavuot, according to the tradition of Moses and Israel, this lengthy letter, as well as the time you spend reading it, will have been well worth the while.

Subsequently, Eli Wiesel did marry, and he attributed his decision, in part, to the Rebbe's prodding. As he related in an interview, the Rebbe was overjoyed at the news: "The greatest bouquet of flowers I ever received was from the Rebbe for my wedding. He was [always] nudging me to get married. I have letters—one letter in which we speak about Jewish theology—seven, eight pages about theology. At the end [of the letter], he said, 'And by the way, when are you getting married?' As if the two had something in common."[119]

In the Rebbe's mind, they clearly did.[120]

In addition to the practical, demographic response, the Rebbe also advocated a *spiritual* retaliation of sorts as a response to the massive loss the Jewish people experienced at the hands of our enemies.

What follows is an excerpt from an informal discussion session between members of the Young Leadership Cabinet of the U.J.A. (United Jewish Appeal) and the Rebbe, which lasted through the evening of March 4, 1962.

> **Question**: We are going on a pilgrimage to commemorate the Warsaw Ghetto uprising, going to Warsaw and Auschwitz. As we get deeper and deeper in the reading, we're all having many problems with the questions that the Holocaust and Auschwitz bring.... What did the whole thing mean?
>
> **Rebbe:** ...if history teaches us something that we must not repeat or must emulate, the best lesson can be taken from the destruction of the Second Temple. We witnessed something so terrible, it must bring every Jew to become more identified with his Jewishness...every one of us has an obligation to fight Hitler, [which] can be done by letting that which Hitler had in mind to annihilate, not only continue, but grow bigger and on a deeper scale. Hitler was not interested so much in annihilating the body of Jewishness as he was interested in annihilating the spirit. [He

decreed that the spiritual and moral ideas which the Jewish people embodied[121]] must not infect the German people, the Russian people, or the Polish people—and because of that, he had all the Polish, Russian, and German people on his side. They regarded the Jews as a foreign body, and a body that does not belong must be eliminated.

If you influence a Jew not to become assimilated but to profess his Jewishness, his pride and inspiration and joy, this is defeating Hitlerism. If someone does his best in his personal life to be Jewish [so that] everyone sees that in the street he is a Jew, that his home is a Jewish home, that he is proud, and that it is not a burden, but his pride, his life defeats the idea of Hitlerism.

When you go to Auschwitz, you must profess there that Auschwitz cannot happen again. You can assure it by becoming a living example of a living Jew. It has nothing to do with chauvinism. You are not trying to convert anyone to be a Jew, but you are fighting, you are struggling for survival not only as a human being, but as a Jew. In our time, it is a very acute problem, because every one of us must do something not only to perform his task but to replace all those Jews that were murdered and annihilated. Their tasks are our direct duty.[122]

In the years following the Holocaust, the Rebbe often expressed the idea that after the German atrocities, which annihilated nearly a third of the Jewish people, every living Jew counts as two, for through each Jew, those who were murdered live on.

The responsibility of survivors and those not directly affected by a catastrophe to represent those who perished is captured in the following story:

A Holocaust survivor once came to see the sixth Lubavitcher Rebbe, Rabbi Yosef Yitzchak Schneersohn, some years after he settled in America. This survivor was plagued by an all-consuming guilt, the type that afflicted many who saw their peers killed off or who were the sole remnant of their entire families or towns. The question of "Why me?" devoured their waking hours. "Why did I survive while the others did not?" they probed others and accused themselves.

This man, too, was haunted by survivor's guilt. He had visited many rabbis for counsel so that he could move on, but to no avail. His search brought him to 770 Eastern Parkway for an audience with the Rebbe.

"What *zechut* (merit) did I have over the others?" he asked desperately. "Why did *I* merit surviving?"

The emphatic two-word response turned his life around: *Zechut? Chov!* ("Merit? Obligation!")

CHAPTER 19

MEASURE FOR MEASURE

An essential theme that comes up in the Rebbe's discussions about "retaliation against evil" is a sort of poetic justice—appropriate action on the part of the survivors that matches the nature, and even the geographical location, of the tragedy.

Following a horrific car accident in Israel that took five lives, the Rebbe reacted by saying: "The way to combat incomprehensible loss and destruction is to counter it with behavior that is similarly incomprehensible—with irrational goodness."[123]

Extending this idea to include the *place* of loss and destruction, the Rebbe wrote to a Mrs. Leah Chein, whose husband had recently passed away:

> I was pleased to learn that the class which started before your husband's passing is in continuance and takes place in the very same place and is based on the very same topics as it was while he was alive.... This is a tremendous advantage for

the soul of the departed and gives it great satisfaction when the good it was involved with continues in the very same location.[124]

On the last day of *shivah*, the seven-day mourning period, for his wife of sixty years, Rebbetzin Chaya Mushka, of blessed memory, the Rebbe made a similar point upon concluding the prayer service when he said: "It is customary to elevate the soul of the deceased through a Chasidic *farbrengen* or gathering. It should be done beautifully and should be held here, in the house where she lived."[125]

Likewise, the Rebbe wrote to Mrs. Fradel Zilberstrom (quoted in chapter 3) regarding the construction of the new school in Kfar Chabad, stating that there is added value in the fact that the school was being built on the very spot where the atrocity was committed.

In a letter to Rabbi Raphael Nachman Kahan, a town elder, the Rebbe writes:

> It goes without saying that you should utilize your strength and employ all of your energy toward encouraging and uplifting the spirits of the townspeople, bearing in mind that especially in a place where cruelty was committed, there should be an outpouring of compassion.[126]

The Rebbe made a similar point to the brothers of

Simcha Zilberstrom, of blessed memory, the teacher who was killed in the attack, when they wrote to him asking what do with the money that Simcha had left behind. The Rebbe suggested that after distributing a symbolic amount to every family member in order to establish the spiritual connection to the deceased that comes with inheritance, "the bulk of his assets should go toward a local organization, particularly one that deals with education (as he did), such as a summer camp or venue for continued education. It would be fitting that prayerbooks be purchased for Simcha's entire class or school from that money."[127]

In a similar vein, the Rebbe guided the family of Avraham Goldman, a seventeen-year-old yeshiva student who had been brutally murdered by three hooligans in an anti-Semitic attack while he was making a phone call to strengthen the Jewish identity of a child. The Rebbe suggested to honor Goldman's memory by creating a fund which would help subsidize the costs of summer camp for Jewish children whose families could not afford it, and in this way the Jewish identity of these children would be strengthened.

More than just a form of poetic justice, rebuilding in the place where there was destruction also has great spiritual significance and benefit.

The Tzemach Tzedek, the third Lubavitcher Rebbe, consoled communities whose homes had been destroyed by a fire. In his letter to them,[128] he drew on the wisdom of the Alter Rebbe, the founder of Chabad Chasidism.

A fire had ravaged the home of one of the Alter Rebbe's Chasidim, R. Yosef of Zuravitz, leaving him homeless and destitute. The Alter Rebbe wrote to him as follows[129]:

> I have heard it said by saintly men, and it has become a common expression, that "after a fire, one becomes wealthy." The logic behind this statement is that on High, the hierarchy of the Divine attributes is *Chesed, Din, Rachamim* [Kindness, Judgment, Mercy]. Therefore, subsequent to the harshness you have suffered, there awaits for you a great amount of Divine benevolence superseding even the original first level, that of *Chesed*.

After citing the Alter Rebbe's words, the Tzemach Tzedek continued:

> Therefore, the Alter Rebbe urged R. Yosef to rebuild his ravaged home in the very same place it had been [so that the increased Divine flow of Mercy could revitalize in greater measure the actual place where Judgment had wreaked havoc].
>
> From his holy words, we can derive instruction to your circumstance. Let each person be

strengthened to rebuild their destroyed homes in the very same places they had been, for communal merit surpasses that of the individual to awaken Mercies that they may be strengthened. Thus, each person should help his neighbor, and may G-d who gives strength bless you with all good in all your endeavors.[130]

In the Divine scheme of things, then, disaster can be seen to pave the way for even greater regeneration and blessing than before. This is especially true when it comes to the ability to transform the place of the disaster, in accordance with the teaching of Chasidut that, in essence, darkness is not an entity or force unto itself, rather it is itself an agent of light.

An incredible demonstration of transforming a void left by the loss of life into a positive force for life was illustrated by the Rebbe himself when, on the 25th of Adar (March 14, 1988), only one month after his wife's passing, the Rebbe inaugurated a global Jewish birthday campaign on the day that would have been her 87th birthday, saying:

Here is a suggestion, and it would be of great merit to her soul, that in connection with the ascent of her soul, the following custom should be established: Jews should begin to celebrate their birthdays, [even though] in previous generations this was observed only by certain individuals and in a discreet manner....[131]

To the Rebbe, the most appropriate and noble way to commemorate the loss of life was through the enhancement and celebration of life's birth.

CHAPTER 20

OPTIMISM IN THE FACE OF TRAGEDY

Late one evening in 1971, a debriefing was taking place at the headquarters of Chabad Lubavitch, located at 770 Eastern Parkway. Gershon Ber Jacobson, a journalist and the editor of a Jewish newspaper, had recently returned from the former Soviet Union, having traveled on a mission to deliver religious contraband to the Jews living there who weren't allowed to practice religion openly and to bolster their spirits and morale. Upon his return, he was asked to see the Rebbe to describe all that he had seen and done while on his covert mission.

Throughout the meeting, which lasted through the night, he recounted the extreme challenges and persecution of his fellow Jews behind the "Iron Curtain," of the trials and tribulations Soviet Jewry faced daily in order to live a religious life, and of their deep longing for religious freedom.

With each passing story of hardship, the Rebbe's face fell further, and it was apparent that he was deeply agitated by their struggle and was personally internalizing and absorbing their pain and suffering.

(And then, as the long night concluded and dawn began to break, a ray of sunshine suddenly illuminated the Rebbe's office. Catching sight of the rising sun, the Rebbe slowly stood up, his face transformed from utter exhaustion to radiant vitality, his shoulders relaxed from the heavy weight of Soviet Jewry he carried personally, and, as if welcoming a long-lost friend, he said in a longing voice: *Ah, a nayem tog….* ["Ah, a new day…."][132])

A hallmark of the Rebbe's approach to the world was an almost stubborn optimism in the face of tragedy—a refusal to live in fear or to see our world as anything but inherently good.[133]

In a rare personal disclosure to one of his Chasidim and a confidante, Rabbi Berel Junik, the Rebbe once referred to his focus on seeing things positively as stemming from his past, saying, "I worked on myself to look at things in a positive light, otherwise I could not have survived."

Having lived through pogroms, World War One, a typhus epidemic, the Bolshevik revolution, the rise of Communism, and World War Two, the Rebbe had made a conscious decision to focus on the positive rather than the negative in his life and the world around him.

The following letter was written by the Rebbe to an individual who was wont to complain about his life circumstances.

> I acknowledge receipt of your letter…. Despite its tone and content…I have not, God forbid, lost hope that eventually you will appreciate the good in life, including the good in your own life, and that this appreciation will impact your emotions and frame of mind….In our world, everything is a mixture of good and bad. Human beings must choose which aspects they will emphasize, contemplate, and pursue. In everyone's life there are two paths—to see the good or [the opposite]….
>
> How instructive is that which our Sages tell us, that Adam was an ingrate. Even before he was banished from the Garden of Eden, [while living in a literal paradise,] he complained about his circumstances. On the other hand, there were Jewish men and women who thanked and blessed the Creator and recited the morning blessings while living through the most horrifying times in the German concentration camps. Ultimately, everyone's circumstances will be somewhere between these two extremes….

Needless to say, my intention is not to imply that anyone deserves suffering, God forbid. My point is simply to underscore the reality: The type of lives that we live, whether full of satisfaction and meaning or the opposite, depends, in large measure, on our willpower, which dictates whether we will focus on the positive or on the negative.[134]

In another pointed letter, written to an individual who complained that he had "never experienced goodness in his life," the Rebbe wrote sharply:

> In response to your letter…in which you write about your current situation and that throughout your life you have not experienced any good….
>
> It seems that you do not sense the contradiction in your letter. For a man who G-d has blessed with a wife and children to say that he has never seen any good is ungrateful to an alarming degree…. Hundreds, even thousands, of people pray every day to be blessed with children and would give everything they own to have a single child but have not as of yet merited this….
>
> But you, the recipient of this blessing, which it seems came to you without you having to especially pray for it, don't recognize the wealth and happiness in the blessings you have, and you write twice in your letter that you have never experienced any good![135]

On another occasion, after reading a memoir written by Rabbi Yitzchak Goldin, who had suffered at the hands of the authorities for his actions to spread Judaism during Communist times and who wrote, "All of the days of my life were bad…," the Rebbe wrote to him:

> How can you write that (all of the days of your life were bad)! You learned for six years in Tomchei Temimim (the elite Lubavitcher yeshiva); you assisted my father-in-law, the Rebbe, in his private affairs; you were blessed to fulfill the missions he entrusted you with; you were arrested on account of the noble activities you engaged in to preserve Judaism, and even in prison you were able to continue your Holy work. If after all this you say that all of your life was bad, then I have no idea what good is![136]

On the tenth day of Shevat, January 28, 1950, the Rebbe's father-in-law, the sixth Lubavitcher Rebbe, Rabbi Yosef Yitzchak Schneersohn, returned his soul to his Maker. Few events affected the Rebbe as deeply as the passing of his father-in-law and predecessor, whom he greatly revered. Indeed, there was hardly a talk he gave in the following four decades of his leadership that didn't make mention of "my father-in-law, the Rebbe."

In an address he delivered on the 10th of Shevat,

1972, the Rebbe expounded on a discourse by Rabbi Yosef Yitzchak entitled "I Have Come to My Garden" (based on a verse from the Song of Songs 5:1):

> Here we have a magnificent lesson: The world in which my father-in-law lived—and he conveyed this lesson for the days and years to come—is a veritable garden. It is not just like a field that produces grain; it is a garden that produces fruits.
>
> Furthermore, it is not just anyone's garden, of average value with average fruits, whose owner is satisfied with a mediocre harvest. It is, as the verse stresses, "My garden." G-d says that our world is His personal orchard.
>
> Moreover, it is not of secondary importance to him; it is "My abode"—the very essence of G-d dwells in this world. So whether we understand how this is or not, the Torah of truth says it is so, that we live in a world, regardless of how it may appear to the physical eye, that is a garden.
>
> This allows one to look at the world differently. From this perspective, one can see that which on the surface, and at first glance, one did not notice.
>
> This is the lesson that my father-in-law, the Rebbe, imparted on the day of his passing for us[137] to take along for all the years: despite evil attempts to conceal the preciousness of our world, and for us to give up hope, heaven forbid…we must know that we are in a precious world![138]

While it is certainly necessary to exercise caution and act with a reasonable sense of safety, our overall approach to the world should not be one of fear and mistrust. Rather, we should meditate on and remember that the true nature of the world is that it is beautiful and precious.

Of all the quotes of the Rebbe included in this book, it is the next one that I include with the greatest sense of caution, lest it come across, G-d forbid, as insensitive or be taken out of context. It is a point that may be hard to digest emotionally, even if it is intellectually sound. But ultimately, I have chosen to include it, as it addresses an important perspective on personal loss in particular and Jewish history in general.

On the individual level, it speaks to those whom, upon experiencing loss and sorrow, cease to see the world in the way they did prior to suffering loss. They are forever marked by tragedy and have come to define themselves by their pain. Worse yet, their life story is seen and experienced through the prism of sadness and grief, which holds them back from living and loving fully again.

On the collective level of Jewish history, the Rebbe's words address the typical post-Holocaust victim-narrative of Jewish history, which emphasizes the many persecutions Jews suffered at the hands of their enemies, in other words, how Jewish people lost, rather than lived, their lives throughout history.

In a public address given on April 13, 1973,[139] the Rebbe, who rarely spoke about the Holocaust publicly, shared the following perspective:

> A fundamental principle to consider: If you ask a thinking person, "Can a spear or sword harm something spiritual?", they would laugh at the question because the two have no connection. What ability does a sword or spear have—or fire or water, for that matter—to damage something spiritual?
>
> Everyone knows that fire can injure only the body and may sever the connection between body and soul, but it can burn the soul no more than water can drown it....
>
> And if you were to ask a rational individual, what is the person's essence? Persons whom he loves, whom he is close with, his father or his mother, what are they truly, the body or soul? They will say that the person is the soul! And even though they are made of flesh and blood, etc., and he connects with them physically through touching them and speaking to them, but with whom is he really connected?
>
> Who [or what] is it that is [really] precious to him? Whom does he defend? Whose pain is he

alarmed about? The souls of the beloved person with whom he has a connection…. This soul, even when it was sent to Auschwitz, and it gave his/her life for being a Jew, [only] the body was taken, but the soul remains. [It is] the connection between body and soul [that] may have been broken, but the soul lives on. The soul remains the day after Auschwitz, a year after Auschwitz, and a generation after Auschwitz…. The soul remains whole. How long does it remain whole? There is no reason to say that any changes in this world affect the soul. There is no reason to say that the soul ever ceases to exist.

What does this principle tell us?

If someone were to come and report, "I met a person for a moment, and that person was crying; it must be that his entire life was full of incredible and unbearable pain! How do I know this? Because at the moment that I saw him, he was crying; he was screaming in terrible pain!" Or if he reports the opposite, "I met someone at one time, and he was full of great elation, so his life must be one long story of joy and happiness, without any pain whatsoever!" Such a person would be called a fool. The fact that you observed one moment, out of a person's 120 years of life, does not indicate in any way the story of that person's entire life, past or future.

So too, those who perished in Auschwitz lived a certain number of years up to that point, and thereafter, their souls [continue to] live on for thousands of years to come…. [It's true that] we saw the person for a [terrible pain-filled] moment, [but] compared to the soul's eternal life, [it] was less than a passing moment in 120 years.

[Therefore,] it is illogical to conclude, by observing one minute of the soul's eternal life, that this unequivocally proves what the soul is feeling for eternity….

As pertains to us: all the questions that are asked about the Second World War, how it could happen and how it reflects on the eternal existence of the Jewish people, it is similar to observing a person's life for a single moment and judging from this how his life was and will always be….[140]

The essential point here is that it is crucial to put things into perspective and context when analyzing the quality of our personal lives and that of Jewish history in its entirety. And thus, when we take a step back from our current reality and reflect on that which preceded and that which will follow our immediate lifespan, and similarly when we take into account the entire lifespan of the Jewish people, we come to see the pain and tragedy we may suffer in our life and the suffering throughout Jewish history as fleeting and but a finite speck compared to the joy, abundance, and longevity we experienced as a nation and as individuals with eternal souls.

By de-emphasizing the colossal loss and destruction to Jewish life created by the Holocaust as the central point of national focus and self-definition, the Rebbe chose not to devalue or trivialize that loss, Heaven forbid, but to ensure that it not come to define and confine the way the Jewish people view their past, present, and future.

And on an individual level, upon encountering crushing loss or tragedy, the Rebbe's words serve as an inspiration and an invitation to uproot and replace a paralyzing life-narrative infused with pain and suffering with the broader and more liberating view on life that takes the whole picture into account, including the soul's eternally blissful existence that long preceded and will long continue after our brief physical stay on earth.

CHAPTER 21

FAITH IN THE SUPREMACY OF GOOD OVER EVIL

With the recent rise of terrorism in many parts of the world, it is hard to be optimistic; indeed, it is only natural to wonder whether we're approaching a very dangerous period in history. This concern is especially pertinent in our advanced era of technology and communication, which turns our world into a global village. The faces of terror have become so diverse and the acts of atrocity so creative and bold, and all the while they are striking closer and closer to home, making us wonder: "Are we truly safe anywhere? Are the forces of evil gaining the upper hand? Is our world headed for disaster?"

As illustrated by the following anecdote, the Rebbe strongly emphasized that the ultimate victory is in the hands of the righteous, not in the hands of the physically strong. As history has proven time and again, goodness and justice do prevail.

On June 27, 1976, an Air France plane en route from Paris to Tel Aviv was hijacked by Palestinian and German terrorists and diverted to Entebbe Airport in Uganda. The hijackers separated the Jewish passengers from the others and threatened to kill them if their demands were not met. Israel's government offered to negotiate in order to stall for time. A week later, the world awoke to stunning headlines. The hostages were safe and sound and back in their homeland after a miraculous, death-defying raid by Israeli Special Forces, 2,500 miles from home.

At a public address two weeks later, the Rebbe spoke about the lessons that could be learned from this spectacular rescue operation:

> From time to time, we are granted the opportunity to actually see in this physical world how quality can prevail over quantity.... This brings us to the recent astonishing event which shook the entire world. We refer, of course, to the miraculous rescue of dozens of Jewish hostages from death to life and their safe return to a civilized land.
>
> There was no natural way of seeing how it could be done. And yet we saw with our own eyes how quality prevailed over quantity. The enemies greatly outnumbered the rescuing forces—both at the airport itself, and even more so, if you count all the enemy forces in all the countries that had

to be flown over in order to rescue the hostages and then again on their return to the Holy Land.

And in the operation itself: it wasn't quantity that won; it wasn't the number of weapons or men that determined who prevailed. On the contrary, the force with fewer men and weapons was victorious; it was the quality of the liberators that prevailed over the quality of the captors.

Moreover [regarding] the rescuers themselves, their own "quality" prevailed over their own "quantity." In terms of quantity—that is, their physical considerations—there should have been no way for people to allow themselves to participate in such a mission. What they did goes against the body's nature, the basic instinct for self-preservation, which would normally prevent a person from getting involved in this whole [operation] from the start. However, since spiritual considerations prevailed—and not just spiritual considerations but the spiritual instinct that transcends all consideration—they allowed themselves to do what they did.[141]

While the media consistently reinforces the image of a world that is falling apart, where brutality and strength prevail, it is important to remember that goodness—no matter how tenuous and fragile it may seem—has the power to triumph.

CHAPTER 22

TRAGEDY AS A WAKE-UP CALL

Notwithstanding his optimistic view of our world as a divine garden of essential goodness, the Rebbe was not blind to the fact that oftentimes, our world on its surface conducts itself not as the divine garden it inherently is but as a jungle. The Rebbe urged that our response to humanly generated tragedies must include the taking of concrete steps to improve the moral state of society.

On Monday, March 30, 1981, just sixty-nine days into his presidency, US President Ronald Reagan was leaving a speaking engagement at the Washington Hilton Hotel in Washington, D.C., when he was shot. The president suffered a punctured lung, but with prompt medical attention, he recovered quickly.

On April 15th of that year, at a community gathering marking his birthday (on the 11th of the Hebrew month of Nissan), the Rebbe addressed the recent attempt on the president's life and shared the following lesson with the thousands who were gathered for the event:

> How could it happen that a person (the would-be assassin) should take such incomprehensible action that contradicts all reason and sensibility? Historically it has been argued that the root of all crime is poverty, which embitters the human spirit and, in turn, leads to feelings of revenge....
>
> We see in the present case that the person who attempted the assassination was not at all impoverished—to the contrary, he was raised amid wealth[142] and, apparently, he was denied nothing. Lest it be argued that poverty is the root of crime, this incident makes clear that to find the root cause of such deplorable actions we cannot look to the person's economic background, but somewhere else.
>
> Where can the root cause be found? The present case points us in its direction: education....
>
> It is true that, by law, schooling is obligatory, but what is the philosophy of the public education system? What is expected of the schools? Only to transmit knowledge, not to shape, cultivate, or structure the child's inner self—that he develop good character traits and that he recognize that, with all the facts he learns at school, the most important thing to learn is how to do good.[143]

In this talk, the Rebbe reiterated a position he had advocated many times, including his letter to then Vice President Walter F. Mondale (9th of Shevat, 5739 [February 26, 1979]):

> Education, in general, should not be limited to the acquisition of knowledge and preparation for a career, or, in common parlance, "to make a better living." We must think in terms of a "better living" not only for the individual but also for the society as a whole. The educational system must, therefore, pay more attention, indeed the main attention, to the building of character, with emphasis on moral and ethical values.

A more sharply worded iteration of this message can be found in a letter written by the Rebbe to Chaplain Brigadier General Israel Drazin in 1987:

> Many thanks for the good news [your letter] contained, particularly about your talks and lectures on the Seven Noahide Commandments[144] on a number of occasions and that these were well received, even enthusiastically. I am certainly gratified that you intend to continue doing so.
>
> There is, of course, no need to emphasize to you the importance of promoting these Seven Noahide Commandments among gentiles. In our day and age, it does not require much imagination to realize that, by way of example, had

these Divine Commandments been observed and adhered to by all the "Children of Noah," namely, the nations of the world, individually and collectively, there would not have been any possibility, in the natural order of things, for such a thing as a Holocaust.[145]

In 1964, the acclaimed American novelist Harvey Swados visited the Rebbe for a *yechidut.* In the course of their meeting, during which they discussed Hannah Arendt's recently published book entitled *Eichmann in Jerusalem: A Report on the Banality of Evil,* in which she accused the Jewish leadership during the Holocaust of having acquiesced too easily to the Nazis' horrific demands, the Rebbe took a different approach, highlighting the incredible difficulties of retaining one's integrity under totalitarian regimes. "…the miracle was that there was any resistance at all, that there was any organization at all, that there was any leadership at all."

Swados then asked the Rebbe pointedly whether it was his opinion that the tragedy of the Holocaust was not a unique visitation upon the Jewish people and that it could happen again? Without hesitation, the Rebbe replied, *Morgen in der frie,* "Tomorrow morning."

Swados asked: "Why [are you] so certain that so terrible a horror could occur again?" According to Swados,

"The Rebbe launched into an analysis of the German atrocities…. He did not speak mystically nor did he harp on the German national character and its supposed affinity for Jew-hatred. Rather, he insisted upon the Germans' obedience to authority and their unquestioning carrying out of orders—even the most bestial—as a cultural-historical phenomenon that was the product of many generations of deliberate inculcation."[146]

The point the Rebbe made was that a society that does not inculcate in its citizens a belief in a Higher Power Who demands righteous and moral behavior could, if it had the military power to do so, carry out genocide against any ethnic group.

Just as the Rebbe saw the individual tragedies that occur in people's lives as a call for *teshuvah*, the Rebbe's response to national and global "man-made" tragedy was that it was a call upon society to reflect on its values and policies. The Rebbe was especially concerned about the state of education for youth, which he felt must include character development and moral education in order to ensure a safe and healthy society. Through proper education for all, the Rebbe felt, we could effectively transform our world from a "jungle" into a "garden."

CHAPTER 23

MAINTAINING CALM IN THE FACE OF DANGER

Taking his cue from Moses, the ultimate Jewish leader, the Rebbe also taught that it was the responsibility of Jewish leaders to maintain calm in the face of calamity.

When the new Jewish nation was advancing toward the Promised Land, Balak, king of Moab, heard about the approach of the Jewish army and began to panic and sow seeds of fear among his people:

> Moab was very frightened of the [Jewish] people…so frightened that they "were disgusted with their own lives!" …Moab said to the elders of Midian: "Now the [Jewish] congregation will chew up our entire surroundings, as an ox chews up the greenery of the field!"[147]

Moses had faced a similar fear not long before this when he had to do battle with Og, king of Bashan: "Moses was afraid to wage war lest the merit of Abraham stand on Og's behalf."[148] And yet, the Rebbe points out[149] that although Moses was also afraid, his response was radically different. He assumed an air of tranquility and confidence, which spread throughout his people and helped them win the war.

In the winter of 1955, Yisroel Aryeh Dobruskin made his way from the yeshiva in Lod, Israel, to the vocational school in the village of Kfar Chabad, where he served as spiritual mentor. Tragically, he never arrived at his destination. A few days later, his body was found in a nearby orchard. He had been brutally murdered by Arab terrorists, who were lying in wait in the orchard.

Immediately upon hearing of the tragedy, the Rebbe sent a letter to Mr. Zalman Shazar (who would later become Israel's third president), expressing his concern about the emotional and psychological impact the terrorist attack would likely have on local residents of Kfar Chabad. In the letter, he urged Shazar to take action that would calm the rampant fears and feelings of insecurity:

> I just received the shocking news that one of our finest yeshiva students [studying] in our yeshiva in Lod was found murdered in the orchard near the library, may G-d avenge his blood....
> What urged me to write to you so soon is my concern about the profound and traumatic impact this tragic event will leave on the residents

of the neighboring village of Kfar Chabad…and the negative consequences that might ensue as a result.

It is imperative that everything possible be done to bring a spirit of calm and security to the residents, which can be achieved through the involvement and efforts of the local agencies….

It seems to me that one of the ways to create a sense of stability and security would be to expand the number of residents living in the Kfar….

I would like to emphasize again that, in my opinion, if the residents of the Kfar would receive information that [governmental] efforts have begun to expand the population of the Kfar, a measure of calm, if only a small measure, will help to still their turbulent, fearful emotions.[150]

A year and a half later, the Rebbe acted on his own advice. Shortly after a terrorist attack on a school in Kfar Chabad (see chapters 12 and 14) that took the lives of five of its students, the Rebbe announced his intention to send a delegation "to show solidarity not just in pocket[151] but in body."[152] Within the month, a group of rabbinical students were chosen for the mission, and they left within days of their appointment.

Nowhere was the Rebbe's commitment to defusing frightening situations and spreading calm more evident than in his consistent message to Israeli citizens and world Jewry during the many tense periods when they faced grave danger. He was often the lone voice of calm and reassurance during periods of heightened panic and among a cacophony of frantic voices predicting doom.[153]

An example: On May 22, 1967, Egypt's president, Gamal Abdel Nasser, declared the Straits of Tiran closed to all Israeli ships and to any foreign ships carrying strategic materials to the Jewish state in violation of international agreements, an act that constituted legal grounds to declare war. In the face of the growing fear that spread throughout Israel, the Rebbe sent an encouraging telegram the following day to the Chabad community in Israel, saying: "You have merited to be among thousands of Jews in the Holy Land, the land which G-d's eyes are constantly watching (Deuteronomy 11:12). Certainly the Lord of Israel will not slumber nor sleep…I am anticipating hearing good news quickly."[154]

Over the coming weeks, the Rebbe wrote many such letters and made many public pronouncements to the same effect.

The uniqueness of the Rebbe's message of reassurance during that terrifying period can be gleaned from the fact that it was featured in many of the major Israeli newspapers under the title, "Lubavitcher Rebbe Sends Letter of Encouragement."[155]

Over the next few weeks, the rhetoric emanating out of the Arab world grew especially fierce, with Nasser proclaiming on May 27, "Our basic objective will be the destruction of Israel."

Jews around the world were beginning to despair with each passing day and its accompanying bad news. More Arab governments were broadcasting their readiness to join in the war.

In a country in which a large portion of the population was comprised of survivors of the Holocaust, many felt that another Holocaust might be imminent. Rabbinic authorities, anticipating the possibility of horrific losses, prepared for the prospect of turning parks into giant cemeteries that could hold twenty-five thousand bodies or more.

Many foreign-born Jews used their non-Israeli passports to leave Israel for safer dwellings elsewhere. The Rebbe instructed his followers not to so. Throughout the terrifying three weeks that preceded the war, the Rebbe proclaimed again and again that Israel would emerge from the upcoming conflict with a great victory.

Perhaps the most significant speech of encouragement was the one the Rebbe delivered on May 28 at the 1967 Lag B'Omer parade in Crown Heights, just a week before the Six-Day War began.

Addressing more than twenty thousand people, the Rebbe spoke forcefully and passionately about the expected conflict in Israel. Without hesitation, he predicted yet again: "G-d is guarding Israel and…the people of Israel will emerge from the current situation with remarkable success."[156]

In Israel, a taped version of the Rebbe's speech was broadcast on national radio, with simultaneous translation from Yiddish to Hebrew. One major newspaper headline quoted the Rebbe's address, reading, "G-d is already protecting the Holy Land, and salvation is near." The news article spoke of the Rebbe's displeasure with the overwrought atmosphere engulfing much of the country: "I am displeased with the exaggerations being disseminated and the panicking of the citizens in Israel."[157]

Within two weeks, the Rebbe's optimistic prediction of salvation came true, with Israel miraculously vanquishing its enemies in just six days! A country that had faced destruction had become universally recognized as the greatest military power in the Middle East.

In 1971, Rabbi Mordechai Piron succeeded Rabbi Shlomo Goren as chief rabbi of the IDF—a position he would hold two years later during the Yom Kippur War, when he had the dubious distinction of informing families that their loved ones had fallen and overseeing the burial of the many casualties. Reflecting on that dreadful loss of life, Piron has said he has never been fully joyful since then.

During the war, he recalled, "I kept a constant phone connection with the Rebbe through his secretariat. The Rebbe would encourage me. More than once I would receive a midnight call from the Rebbe telling us to be happy, as joy sweetens the most severe decrees. Given the terrible morale in the army—especially in the high command—the Rebbe's words lightened our load…it gave me the feeling of someone placing his hand on my shoulders whispering, 'Move on, don't fall apart.'"[158]

The message about a leader's responsibility to maintain tranquility applies to parents as well.

> There was once a young girl from a very poor family who was having terrifying dreams. Her parents consulted a rabbi about this problem. He said: "The Sages say that we dream at night what we think about during the day. Ask your daughter what she is afraid of."
>
> When they asked her, she replied: "I often see how you both sit and worry over the poverty we live in. Of everything, I am most afraid of your fear."[159]

CHAPTER 24

THE PROTECTIVE POWER
OF MITZVOT

In addition to being an example of a leader who took
responsibility for his community and prompted other
leaders to do the same, the Rebbe, by word and example, urged anyone in a position of influence to promote
and inspire added mitzvah observance in the face of
tragedy. In particular, when it came to catastrophes
where individual safety and national security were com-
promised, the Rebbe promoted the observance of those
mitzvot that possess special protective properties, like
mezuzah and *tefillin*.

Just before the outbreak of the Six-Day War in 1967,
when the people of Israel seemed in great peril in face
of the murderous intentions and rhetoric of its hostile
neighbors, the Rebbe initiated his famed "*tefillin* campaign." Noting that the Sages of the Talmud attributed
to *tefillin* the quality of protecting the people of Israel
from their enemies,[160] the Rebbe instructed his followers

to make every effort to get as many Jews to fulfill this mitzvah. As a result of this campaign, hundreds of thousands of Jews donned *tefillin*, many for the first time in their lives.

In the months leading to the outbreak of the Yom Kippur war in 1974, the Rebbe urged that gatherings be arranged where Jewish children would recite words of Torah and pray, citing the verse from the book of Psalms that attributes the power to "annihilate the enemy and avenger" to the sacred word issuing from the mouths of children.[161] During the war itself, the Rebbe urged Rabbi Piron to ensure that all army bases had kosher *mezuzahs*. Rabbi Piron issued an order that Chabad Chasidim were to be given full access to all installations, where they brought *tefillin*, words of faith, and messages of encouragement from the Rebbe.

In another example, in 1981, months before the Lebanon War, the Rebbe requested that a Torah scroll be written specifically for members of the IDF and their families. When the war actually broke out, the Rebbe conveyed to the Lubavitcher rabbis in Israel that they extend every effort to ensure that the Torah be completed as soon as possible. The Rebbe later commented that the expedited completion of the Torah scroll had a direct correlation to the safety and security of the soldiers who had fought in the war.[162]

Following the successful hostage-rescue mission undertaken by the IDF in July of 1976, after a plane carrying many Israeli passengers was hijacked and diverted to the Entebbe airport in Uganda, the Rebbe wrote the following pastoral letter to his followers around the world:

> In view of the recent events—the hijacking and saving of the hostages held in Uganda and the subsequent attempt of the terrorists to perpetrate a vicious reprisal, G-d forbid, in Kushta (Istanbul)....
>
> It should be understood that these events are an indication that Jews must, at the earliest possible opportunity, strengthen all aspects of their security and defenses—first and foremost in their spiritual life, which is the channel to receive G-d's blessings as well in the physical aspect...to be protected and secured from enemies and spared any undesirable happenings, G-d forbid....
>
> The present situation calls for the protection of every Jewish home...G-d has given our people a special gift wherewith to protect the home, namely, the mitzvah of *mezuzah*. Our Sages declare explicitly that "the home is protected by it (the *mezuzah*)."[163]

On May 15, 1974, three armed Palestinian terrorists entered Israel from Lebanon and attacked a van, killing two Israeli Arab women. They then entered an apartment building in the town of Ma'alot, where they killed a couple and their four-year-old son. From there, they headed for the Netiv Meir elementary school, where they took more than 115 people (105 of them children) hostage. The hostage-takers soon issued demands for the release of twenty-three Palestinian militants from Israeli prisons. On the second day of the standoff, a unit of the Golani Brigades stormed the building. During the takeover, the hostage-takers killed some of the children with grenades and automatic weapons. Ultimately, twenty-five hostages, including twenty-two children, were killed, and sixty-eight more were injured.

After a period of intense mourning, the Rebbe issued a call for action. He urged Jewish leaders to join a worldwide *mezuzah* campaign, aimed at securing every Jewish home with an extra measure of protection. The Rebbe clarified that:

> This is not to say, heaven forbid, that a *mezuzah*-less home or an unkosher *mezuzah* is a *cause* of harm. Heaven forbid saying such a thing! However, like a helmet at war, a *mezuzah* adds protection to the "bullets" of life. If someone who wasn't wearing a helmet was hit by a bullet, G-d

forbid, it's the bullet, not the lack of helmet that harmed him. It's just that were he wearing the helmet, catastrophe could have been averted.[164]

CHAPTER 25

COMMUNAL PEACE AS A BULWARK AGAINST TRAGEDY

In 1958, after a resident from Kfar Chabad, a village in central Israel, passed away, the Rebbe wrote a letter to their community council, which alluded to a link between the recent loss and an act of violence committed by one of the townspeople against another.

> In connection with the undesirable episode that recently took place involving aggression, etc.... I felt the need to write to you about the shocking effects of such an episode:
>
> It is easily observable that since the establishment of Kfar Chabad [in 1949], a special measure of Divine protection prevailed...to the degree that not a single resident of the village had passed away in the interim! The miraculous nature of this phenomenon is self-evident. But since a revelation of Divine compassion requires an appropriate "vessel," and the "vessel" most conducive to

G-d's blessing is peace, especially as the leaders of Chabad, in whose spirit the village was founded, gave their lives for the sake of loving their fellow Jew, it is therefore obvious that all residents of the village should take great care to engender peace, unity, and brotherhood….

P.S. Based on the words of the Sages regarding [trying to avert] the negative effects that occur to someone else [who has wronged you], those who were wronged should take upon themselves to increase their mitzvah observance, and it goes without saying to uproot and eradicate any hard feelings they may bear [against those who wronged them], G-d forbid, G-d forbid….[165]

Here, too, the Rebbe made clear that the act of violence was not the *cause* of death, G-d forbid, but that the previous absence of disunity had been the merit which ensured a special measure of protection.

The premium that the Rebbe placed on unity and peace was a trademark of his worldview in general.

In 1987, a yeshiva student was traveling by car when his vehicle was struck by a truck, resulting in a terrible accident which severely injured the young man.[166]

That Shabbat,[167] during his address, the Rebbe made reference to the tragedy and said that the way to facilitate Divine blessing and protection is through engendering peace and harmony among G-d's children.[168]

He addressed this issue in a letter he wrote to the residents of Kfar Chabad in the aftermath of a massacre that took place there. At the time, doubts about the town's future fueled much dispute:

> It is obvious, and this is the most fundamental point of all, that the spirit of camaraderie and brotherhood among yourselves must increasingly be nurtured and strengthened…. Even if one strongly believes that his viewpoint is the correct one, and even if, objectively, this is indeed the case, nonetheless, it is more important that he "pass over his emotions," for the ideal of peace is a tremendous virtue, one which draws down and retains G-d's infinite blessings and has the power to make them tangible and manifest in our reality.[169]

It is only natural that following a loss—especially when it comes to terrorism, which intensifies feelings of insecurity and vulnerability—emotions and passions run high. The result can be friction and confrontation between opinion-holders and decision-makers.

The Rebbe taught that especially after a communal tragedy, it is important that leaders maintain a clarity of purpose, steering their communities toward rebuilding as a cohesive unit, emphasizing the importance of camaraderie and unity as a vehicle for divine blessing, as is highlighted in the words of the *Amida* prayer, *Barchenu avinu kulanu ke'echad*, "Bless us, Heavenly Father, [*for*] we are one."

CHAPTER 26

REFUSING TO JUSTIFY TRAGEDY

While the Rebbe always insisted that we take tragic events to heart, using them as catalysts for spiritual reflection and growth (see chapter 11 above), he also rejected summary "explanations" for tragic events.

On several occasions and in different contexts, the Rebbe spoke out against those who sought to blame disasters—either impending ones or those already visited upon the nation of Israel—on a lack of Torah observance. As was his wont, the Rebbe went to great lengths not only to view his fellow Jews positively but to find reasons for their behavior, even if it was at times flawed.

Repeatedly, the Rebbe stressed that G-d loves His children—as the Torah states over and over[170]—and that He does not wish to hear derogatory words about them. Even the prophets, of whom it is said that "the spirit of the G-d spoke through them, and His word was on their tongue,"[171] were warned that "G-d does not desire one who speaks badly of His people."[172]

Nowhere was the Rebbe's defense of the Jewish people—and his adamant insistence that they be viewed with a loving eye—more pronounced than when he spoke about the Holocaust. In 1990, as tensions increased in the Persian Gulf and Iraq was threatening Israel with chemical warfare, there was one influential Israeli rabbi who claimed (in a speech that was published in the Israeli media) that the impending war would be another Holocaust, which, as its predecessor, would be a punishment for the abandonment of religious practice. The Rebbe's response to this claim was strong and unequivocal:

> This generation, the remnant of the Holocaust in which six million Jews (may G-d avenge their blood) were killed, may be compared to a "smoldering ember rescued from the flames." G-d forbid, therefore, [that anyone] speak ill of them to the extent as to warn them of another holocaust!... Such an outburst against this generation is made sevenfold worse when it is connected with desecrating the honor of those who died in the Holocaust by stating that the Holocaust happened because of their sins....[173]

Instead, the Rebbe reiterated what he had said on

numerous prior occasions, that there are things that happen in the world not as a punishment for sins, but rather as a result of a Divine decree for which even great Torah scholars cannot find any rationale. For example, who can explain why one of the greatest Sages of the Talmud, Rabbi Akiva, was murdered in such a brutal manner by the Romans or why the "ten martyrs"[174] died in similarly horrific ways. When the Sages sought the answer from G-d, they were only told: "Be silent…"[175] or "It is My decree."[176]

The prime example of such an inexplicable decree is G-d's revelation to Abraham: "Know with certainty that your children shall be strangers in a land not their own. They will be enslaved and oppressed for four hundred years."[177] This decree, said the Rebbe, was not due to any sins, rather it was a Divine decree.[178] And so it is with the Holocaust:

> The destruction of six million Jews in such a horrific manner that surpassed the cruelty of all previous generations could not possibly be because of a punishment for sins. Even the Satan himself could not possibly find a sufficient number of sins that would warrant such genocide! There is absolutely no rational explanation for the Holocaust except for the fact that it was a Divine decree—definitely not the inner will of G-d—rather

a moment when "for a brief moment I (G-d) left you."[179] Why it happened is beyond human comprehension, but it is definitely not because of a punishment for sin. On the contrary—all those who were murdered in the Holocaust are called "holy ones" (*kedoshim*), since they were murdered in sanctification of G-d's Name because they were Jews, and it is only G-d who will avenge their blood.

So great is the spiritual level of the *kedoshim*— even disregarding their standing in mitzvah performance—that the rabbis say about them, "No creation can stand in their place."[180] How much more so [can this be said] of those who died in the Holocaust, many of whom came from the finest of Europe's Torah-observant Jewry, as is well known.

[Therefore,] it is inconceivable that the Holocaust be cited as an example of punishment for sin.[173]

The Rebbe found as particularly reprehensible the idea that G-d sits in heaven calculating the sins of His people in anticipation of punishing them. Such a perspective on the way that G-d conducts the affairs of this world is nothing less than an insult to G-d:

[It is] the opposite of Heavenly honor to describe G-d as one who sits and calculates the number of sins and waits until there is enough to take retribution and then when punishment is exacted, He again starts counting…. This is surely the opposite of respect for G-d, as it gives the impression that G-d can be compared to a cruel king who is waiting to punish. This is, in fact, the opposite of the truth, for G-d is a "Merciful Father," as is explicitly stated in numerous verses, particularly [in the book of Exodus which lists] the "thirteen attributes of mercy…."[181]

Moreover, when the Almighty does punish for sins—after He has been abundantly patient—the punishment is not revenge, rather it is for the good of the person in order to cleanse and purify him from the impurity of the sin. In the words of the Alter Rebbe: "Like a merciful father who is wise and righteous but who strikes his son…like a great and awesome king who himself washes the excrement off his only son out of his great love for him."[182] And since this cleansing is done out of love, it causes pain to G-d, and He also cries out, "Woe to Me…" and "I am with them in their troubles"[183]….

On a separate occasion, the Rebbe spoke passionately about the importance of speaking positively about the Jewish people:

All Jewish people are one single, unified entity…. We must appreciate the importance of speaking positively and the detrimental effects of speaking negatively. Anyone who has true fear of G-d will also fear to speak negatively of His children. Criticizing or speaking unfavorably about any portion of the Jewish people is like making such statements about G-d Himself. It is like one who strikes G-d in the apple of His eye. An attack against any Jew is an attack against G-d. When one speaks, his motives are irrelevant; what matters is how people understood his words. This is certainly the case when such statements are made in public, with great publicity, to the extent that they are publicized even by the secular press and in particular when the person making the statements is a public figure who has influence on others.[184]

In classic form, the Rebbe concluded on a positive note: "Those who were spoken of negatively should know that these words will have no effect on them. On the contrary, G-d will bless them in both material and spiritual matters with good health and long years."[185]

The Rebbe advocated that we emulate the example of those great Jewish leaders in history—Moshe, Aaron, the Baal Shem Tov, and Rabbi Levi Yitzchak of Berditchev[186]—who always sought to find merit in the Jewish people, even when the nation of Israel was at a spiritually low point.

CHAPTER 27

A FAITH-BASED PERSPECTIVE ON TRAGEDY

When tragedy strikes—especially a tragedy of such magnitude as the Holocaust—even those with a strong belief in G-d are often confronted with painful theological questions such as: Is it permitted to question G-d or complain to Him? And if not, where are we to turn to find meaning in disaster? And, if we do find meaning or come to terms with catastrophe, are we in some way justifying suffering?

The Rebbe's stance combines unequivocal faith in G-d on the one hand with uncompromised compassion and allowance for human vulnerability on the other.

This ability to balance both the divine and the human perspective can be seen in the following letter, written by the Rebbe to a family in mourning:

I address these lines to you in the hope that they will bring you some comfort.

To begin with, there are many matters and occurrences that are difficult for the human mind to understand. Among them, there are also such that even if they can be understood intellectually, they are hard to accept emotionally....

A second point to bear in mind is that a human being cannot possibly understand the ways of G-d. By way of a simple illustration: An infant cannot possibly understand the thinking and behavior of a great scholar or scientist, even though both are human beings, and the difference between them is only relative in terms of age, education, and maturity. Moreover, it is quite possible that the infant may someday surpass the scientist, who also started life as an infant. But the difference between a created human being and his Creator is absolute. Therefore, our Sages declare that a human being must accept everything that happens, both those that are obviously good and those that are incomprehensible, with the same positive attitude that "All that G-d does is for the good," even though it is beyond human understanding.[187]

While acknowledging the emotional difficulty of seeing Divine Providence in seemingly senseless events, the Rebbe does still gently encourage that kind of perspective.

A distraught host in whose home a young woman had passed away at a celebration for the completion of a Torah scroll (mentioned in chapter 8) posed the following questions to the Rebbe:

> A) How can it be that a mitzvah such as the writing of a Torah scroll should be the cause of such a tragedy?
>
> B) What lesson must he, the host, derive from the fact that something like this occurred in his home?

The Rebbe's response stresses the fact that G-d's ways are unknowable and at the same time suggests a way to look at the event as being guided by Divine Providence:

> Regarding A):
>
> (1) It is impossible for man, a finite creature, to comprehend all the reasons of the infinite Creator. Indeed, we'd have no way of knowing even some of G-d's reasons, were it not for the fact that G-d Himself told us to seek them out in His holy Torah (Torah meaning "instruction").
>
> (2) According to the Torah, it cannot be that anything negative should result from any of G-d's *mitzvot* (including your Torah scroll); on the contrary, these protect against evil and prevent it.
>
> (3) Each and every individual has been granted a set amount of years of life on earth. It is only in extreme cases that one's deeds can lengthen it

or shorten it (with some terrible sin, etc., G-d forbid).

(4) Based on (1), (2), and (3) above, one can perhaps venture to say that had the departed one (peace unto her) not been invited to the Sefer Torah celebration, she would have found herself, at the onset of her [heart] attack, in completely different surroundings: on the street in the company of strangers; without the presence of a doctor who was both a friend and a religious Jew; without hearing, in her final moments, words of encouragement and seeing the faces of friends and fellow Jews. Can one imagine: (a) the difference between the two possibilities? (b) what a person experiences in each second of her final moments, especially a young, religious woman on the festival in which we celebrate and re-experience our receiving the Torah from the Almighty?![188]

(5) According to the teaching of the Baal Shem Tov—that every event, and its every detail, is by Divine Providence—it is possible that one of the true reasons that Mr. Z. was inspired from Above to donate the Torah scroll, etc., was in order that, ultimately, the ascent of the young woman's soul should be accompanied with an inner tranquility, occurring in a Jewish home—a home whose symbol and protection is the *mezuzah*, which opens with the words, "Hear O Israel, G-d is our G-d, G-d is one."

Regarding B):

(1) Obviously, you and your wife, may you live, have many merits. Without having sought it, you had been granted the opportunity from Above for a mitzvah of the highest order: (a) to ease the final moments of a fellow human being; (b) to take care of a *met* mitzvah[189] until the ambulance arrived. The extreme merit of the latter can be derived from the fact that Torah law obligates a *Kohen Gadol*, the High Priest, on Yom Kippur to leave the "holy of holies" in order to take care of a *met mitzvah*!

(2) Such special merits come with special obligations. In your case, these would include explaining the above to those who might have questions identical or similar to those posed in your letter until they see the event in its true light: a tremendous instance of Divine Providence.[190]

The following story is another example where the Rebbe gently encouraged a mourner to see the Divine Providence in their unfortunate situation.

The mother of a woman who was preparing for her daughter's wedding passed away within a week of the wedding. The woman was brokenhearted and could not bring herself to be joyful in anticipation of her daughter's celebration.

The Rebbe wrote a letter[191] to the woman's friend and asked that she share with her the content of a particular Midrash,[192] which states that immediately after the destruction of the Holy Temple, the soul of Moshiach, the future redeemer of Israel, was born.

The juxtaposition of the Temple's destruction and the birth of Moshiach was not a random coincidence, the Rebbe wrote; rather, it reflected the Divine process. Even when inexplicable suffering is destined to occur, G-d provides a counterbalance and a pathway for consolation. When the Jewish people learned that the soul of their future redeemer (who would usher in the Messianic era of world peace) was born, it gave them the strength to overcome the crushing blow of the Holy Temple's destruction.

Likewise, while it would only be natural to think that the wedding would be ruined because of her recent loss and for her to feel especially sad that her mother would unfortunately not be physically present at the wedding, there is another way to look at her situation: G-d had orchestrated the wedding to be in close proximity to her mother's passing to make it easier for her to cope with the loss—by seeing the growth of her family and the perpetuation of her mother's legacy.

CHAPTER 28

THE BELIEVER'S OUTCRY

While emphasizing the instruction of our Sages to accept that everything "G-d does is for the good," the Rebbe took pains to point out that this does not mean that we are required to justify all that G-d does. That is, even as we pursue the silver lining, it's not for us to explain the cloud away.

In a religious context, this may seem counterintuitive. If everything G-d does is for the good, isn't it our obligation as His loyal subjects to be His "apologists" and "PR team" to find and explain the meaning behind every natural and unnatural disaster that occurs?

The answer from the Rebbe is a most definite "No."

After the 1956 massacre in Kfar Chabad, the Rebbe wrote a letter to the award-winning Israeli writer Eliezer Steinman. In the letter (a portion of which we cited in chapter 14 above), he refers to the story in the book of Leviticus[193] that describes the untimely passing of two of Aaron's sons, Nadav and Avihu, by means of "a

fire [that] came forth from G-d and consumed them."
Subsequently, Moses comforted his brother Aaron,
saying, "Of this did G-d speak when He said, 'I will be
sanctified through those who are nearest Me.'" Aaron
responded to this statement with silence. The Talmud[194]
explains that Moses' cryptic words were meant to
convey the idea that when G-d imposes strict judgment
upon the righteous, He is feared and honored—i.e.,
people say that if such is the fate of the righteous, surely
the punishment of the evil will be much worse. The
Rebbe explained how to look at these verses in light of a
current tragedy:

> Some have wanted to explain the horrible tragedy
> in Kfar Chabad as an example of "I will be sanc-
> tified through those who are nearest Me...." That
> explanation, however, is useless. For in that story,
> too, the explanation is cryptic and incomprehen-
> sible; all we learn from there is that such Divine
> behavior exists, but at the most what we have
> here is a juxtaposition of two incomprehensible
> stories of tragedy, but not an explanation of them.
> Therefore, the situation calls for "And Aaron was
> silent[195]."[196]

At a public gathering in 1974, after a terrible car accident claimed the lives of five beloved residents of Kfar
Chabad, including the town's venerated rabbi, Rabbi

Shneur Zalman Garelik, of blessed memory, the Rebbe said, "My father-in-law once said to someone who was trying to make sense of the Holocaust, 'It's not our business to excuse G-d.'"

These seemingly irreverent words were accompanied by a qualifying declaration of faith:

> It goes without saying that the words spoken do not in any way contradict faith; on the contrary, the complaint itself demonstrates the conviction that there is Someone to complain to, that Someone is responsible for what happens in our world, and that He listens and cares.
>
> And for those who wonder how it is possible to express oneself in such a way ("it's not our business to excuse G-d"), this type of talk is rooted in the Talmud:[197]
>
> "Moses came and prayed, 'The great, powerful, and awesome G-d.'[198] Jeremiah came and said, 'Strangers are croaking in His sanctuary![199] Where [are the displays of] His awesomeness?' and did not mention 'awesome' [in his prayer]. Daniel came and said, 'Strangers are enslaving his children [the Jewish nation, during the seventy-year duration of the Babylonian exile[200]]. Where is His power?' and did not say 'powerful.' [Then] came [the Men of the Great Assembly] and said, 'On the contrary! This is His magnificent display of strength, for He restrains His will all these years

that his people are subjugated, in that He shows a long-suffering countenance to the evil by not punishing them despite the numerous oppressions they decree against His people. And these are indeed the great displays of his awesomeness, because if not for the awe of the nations for the Holy One, Blessed is He, how could one solitary nation survive among the seventy nations of the world?"[201] The Men of Assembly therefore reinstated mention of these attributes in their prayer."

The Talmud asks: "Now, the rabbis—that is, Jeremiah and Daniel, each of whom omitted one of the attributes stated by Moses in his prayer—how did they act thus and abolish the institution that Moses instituted?" And the Talmud answers: "Rabbi Elazar said: 'Because they knew about the Holy One, Blessed is He, that He is truthful and despises falsehood; they therefore would not speak falsehood to Him.'" (Given their position that those attributes were not then manifest, they could not utter them in their prayers, as this would constitute speaking falsehood unto G-d.)

And the same is true, in our instance, that when we see an occurrence that is utterly incomprehensible, we must say the truth, that the matter is utterly incomprehensible…and therefore we cry out![202]

David Rivlin, who was the Israeli Consul General in New York in the early seventies, once shared the content of a visit he had with the Rebbe ten years before, together with Moshe Sharett, the second prime minister of Israel. "At one point," Mr. Rivlin recalled, "the Rebbe said something that was engraved in my memory and moves me until today. We had been discussing Eichmann's capture and trial when Moshe Sharett brought up the Holocaust. The Rebbe said that after the Holocaust, there were certain religious leaders who requested that his father-in-law, the sixth Lubavitcher Rebbe, join them in coming out with a harsh proclamation against those who voiced doubts in G-d following the Holocaust. The sixth Rebbe was vehemently opposed 'because there is a place, especially for the complete believer, to express his lack of understanding, and he has full permission to challenge G-d and ask, "How could You do this?"'[203]

It is this trait of crying out upon encountering human suffering, and the refusal to come to terms with or try to make sense of evil, that distinguishes Judaism's greatest leaders, dating back to our patriarch Abraham. In his heart-wrenching plea for G-d to save the depraved city of Sodom, Abraham challenges G-d, "Will the Judge of all the earth not do justice?"[204]

Later on in Jewish history, Moses would also choose to remain conscious of human suffering and pained by it rather than make peace with G-d's ultimate plan. As one moving interpretation would have it, at the burning bush G-d offered to explain the meaning behind human suffering to Moses—"what is above and what is below"[205]—but Moses refused the offer, as it says, "Moses hid his face."[206] Moses had no desire to understand why people suffer; he had no interest in the justification of pain. As hurtful as it would prove to be, he wanted to forever retain the aspect of his humanity that recoils when another human being suffers.

During one particularly emotional talk that he gave on Hoshaana Rabbah 5744 (September 20, 1983), the Rebbe went so far as to imply that the reason, if it can be called a reason, why human suffering cannot be understood by the human mind is in order to leave human beings with no other way to process and rationalize the pain other than "to cry out to G-d sincerely and from the deepest depths of their heart," demanding that, once and for all, He do away with all pain and suffering by ushering the period of Moshiach and world redemption.

After quoting a mystical text which aims to explain the meaning behind the state of *galut*, or Jewish Exile, that began with the destruction of the Holy Temple and the dispersion of the Jewish people into the Diaspora, the Rebbe said:

Over nineteen hundred years of suffering have passed, and we have still not been redeemed…. Notwithstanding all of the rationales given for that which is gained by the state of exile, the questions remain: G-d is Omnipotent and has no limitations. He could have found a way that avoided all forms of severity, certainly any harshness or suffering….

And we are told to accept on faith—even though it is incomprehensible—that one day we will comprehend and thank G-d for his "harshness…."

…we are told that there is one mystery so profound that it will be revealed only when Moshiach comes, and indeed, there are no answers today!

Why is all this suffering necessary? The Divine presence suffers in exile…every single Jew suffers in exile, and it continues to get worse…. "Each day's suffering is greater than the previous one…."

Evidently, the only explanation for such concealment is that G-d wants man to cry out with the deepest sincerity, "We long for you all day!" If a person were to be able to grasp in any way the "goodness" of exile, he would rationalize the pain and wouldn't cry out for the coming of Moshiach from the depths of his soul, so long as even one small part of his soul reassures him that exile is good….[207]

Certainly, this "crying out to G-d with the deepest sincerity" is how the Rebbe reacted to suffering.

While the Rebbe's general attitude was one of optimism, faith, and joy, and his enthusiasm was infectious and uplifting, on the 9th of Adar I, 5752 (February 13, 1992), the Rebbe publicly expressed his anguish at a local tragedy.

A week earlier, a resident of Crown Heights, Pesha Leah Lapine, a wife and mother of four young children, returned from her routine grocery shopping to her home. Attacked by a man who attempted to violate her, she valiantly tried to fight him off before being stabbed to death. The following day, thousands of Chasidic Jews, headed by the Rebbe, escorted her on her final journey to her resting place. For a long time after the coffin had passed him, the Rebbe stood in the street, his face expressing deep pain.

On the last evening of her *shivah*, the Rebbe addressed the crowd assembled at the Chabad Lubavitch Headquarters in Brooklyn. The Chasidim were stunned by his words, which expressed such intense emotion and distress. The Rebbe was trembling; even the lectern at which he stood was shaking. The following is excerpted from the Rebbe's talk that night:

> What has occurred—an act of open

martyrdom—*is utterly incomprehensible!* There is no one to whom to turn for an explanation. All those present, including myself, are equally confounded. So what do we gain by questioning? The question will remain....

For many years to come—if, G-d forbid, the fulfillment of the prophecy, "Those that lie in the dust will arise and sing"[208] will be delayed—these children will long for their mother. They will recount to their own children their intense longing for their mother; they will tell them that she merited to sanctify G-d's Name....

Enough is enough! Have we not sufficed with all the martyrdom we have experienced until now?

...another day passes, another week passes, another moment passes...and Moshiach still has not come! We say and we think and cry out 'Ad masai!' (How long?) How long must we wait in exile? And yet what do we see happening? For the sanctification of G-d's Name, a Jewish soul is taken away; a mother is taken from her children.

May there be no further need to discuss these matters, for the Redemption will come immediately. "Those that lie in the dust will arise and sing," and those who died *al kiddush Hashem* will merit to be resurrected first. And then this young woman will encounter her children and continue their education with a joyous heart.

May this take place in the immediate future without any delay whatsoever![209]

This is but one of numerous talks where the Rebbe poured out all of his anguish over human suffering and his frustration with the drawn-out exile.

Not only did he never get comfortable in exile, he once exclaimed: "We cannot allow G-d to rest until He actually brings Moshiach!"[210]

This was the essence of the message the Rebbe relayed to Mr. and Mrs. Tauger, whose son had been killed on the Pan American Flight 103, which was blown up in a terrorist attack over Lockerbie, Scotland.

When the grieving couple visited the Rebbe for "Sunday dollars," they were introduced by the Rebbe's secretary as a couple "whose son passed away in the Pan Am disaster last year…and who've come to request a blessing."

The Rebbe responded first by blessing them "from here onward to have only happy tidings for you and your entire family" and then, in response to the question posed by the devastated mother, "How can we live with all that has happened?", the Rebbe said: "After everything that has befallen the whole Jewish people in our generation (referring to the Holocaust), we cannot fathom the [meaning behind] tragedies…." [G-d's] reasons we do not know…but since we've seen what happened…and [that] G-d has not yet responded, the one thing it must [do is] reinforce the demand that it is high time for Moshiach to come…He must answer all the questions…."[211]

As he handed the couple a dollar to be given to charity in England, the Rebbe concluded by blessing them, "May you be spared of any future questions…."

The Rebbe's message to this couple, that their loss should "reinforce the demand that it is high time for Moshiach to come…," was characteristic of what he himself did when left with a sense of the unfathomable rationale behind "G-d's reasons for tragedies," which was to channel and pour his profound anguish and sorrow into heartfelt prayer and a demand from G-d that "it is high time for Moshiach to come."

All the Rebbe's activities were driven by a hope and longing for a world free of pain and evil—the world of the Messianic Era.

In fact, the seed of this all-consuming hope and longing can be found in the Rebbe's early childhood, when, growing up in Soviet Ukraine, the Rebbe was witness to the harsh persecution of his brethren.

In a letter addressed to the second president of Israel, Yitzchak Ben-Zvi, the Rebbe writes:

From the time that I was a child attending *cheder*, and even earlier than that, there began to take form in my mind a vision of the future redemption—the redemption of Israel from its last exile, redemption such as would explicate the suffering, the decrees, and the massacres of exile.[212]

In his letter to Mr. Ben-Zvi, the Rebbe goes on to quote the verse from Isaiah that prophesies that in that future time, "I will thank you, G-d, for having rebuked me..." (Isaiah 12:1). The Rebbe explained that as a child, he yearned for the time when, having received consolation as only the Almighty can offer it, the Jewish people would be able to look back at all the hardships and pain of our long exile and give thanks to G-d, acknowledging that everything that had come to pass was for the good.

And so, when faced with the tremendous suffering in this world, whether it be in a personal, communal, or global tragedy, the Rebbe's passionate advocacy for a better world should inform and inspire our lives and the content of our hearts' desires. For in the words of the Midrash regarding the Messianic Era:

All will be healed. The blind, the deaf, and the dumb, the lame, whosoever has any blemish or disability, shall be healed from all their disabilities.... Death itself shall cease, as it is said (in Isaiah 25:8), "Death shall be swallowed up forever, and G-d shall wipe the tears from every face."[213]

May it be speedily in our days!

APPENDIX

By the Grace of G-d
Tishrei 13, 5728 [October 17, 1967]
Brooklyn, NY

Mr. Ariel Sharon,

Greeting and blessings!

I was deeply grieved to read in the newspaper about
the tragic loss of your tender young son, may he rest
in peace. We cannot fathom the ways of the Creator.
During a time of war and peril you were saved—indeed,
you were among those who secured the victory for our
nation, the Children of Israel, against our enemies, in
which "the many were delivered into the hands of the
few, etc."—and yet, during a time of quiet and in your
own home, such an immense tragedy occurred! But is
not surprising that a created being cannot comprehend
the ways of the Creator, Who infinitely transcends us.
Indeed, we are hardly surprised if a small child cannot
comprehend the ways of a great, venerable, and elderly
sage, even though it is only a finite gulf that separates
them.

Obviously, the above does not come to minimize the hurt and pain in any way. Despite the vast distance between us, I wish to express my sympathies.

At first glance it would appear that we are distant from one another, not only geographically but also—or even more so—in terms of being unfamiliar, indeed unaware, of each other, until the Six-Day War (as it has come to be known), when you became famous and celebrated as a commander and defender of our Holy Land and its inhabitants and as a person of powerful abilities. G-d, blessed be He, shone His countenance upon you and granted you success in your activities—indeed a victory of unexpected proportion.

But on the basis of a fundamental, deeply rooted Jewish principle—namely, that all Jews are kindred—the fame that you received served to reveal something that existed even before, i.e., the interconnectedness of all Jews, whether of the Holy Land or of the Diaspora. It is this interconnectedness that spurred me to write the above words to you and your family.

Another factor that motivated me to write this letter is the tremendous inspiration that you aroused in the hearts of many of our Jewish brethren when you put on *tefillin* at the Western Wall, an act which merited great publicity and echoed powerfully and positively into the various strata of our nation, in places both near and far.

An element of solace—indeed, more than just an element—is expressed in the ritual blessing, hallowed by scores of generations of Torah and tradition among our people:

"May the Omnipresent comfort you among the mourners of Zion and Jerusalem."

At first glance, the connection between the mourner to whom this blessing is directed and the mourners of Jerusalem's destruction appears to be quite puzzling. In truth, however, they are connected. For the main consolation embodied by this phrase is in its inner content, namely: The grief over Zion and Jerusalem is common to all the sons and daughters of our people, Israel, wherever they may be (although it is more palpable to those who dwell in Jerusalem and actually see the Western Wall and the ruins of our Holy Temple than to those who are far away from it; nonetheless, even those who are far experience great pain and grief over the destruction). So too is the grief of a single individual Jew or Jewish family shared by the entire nation. For, as the Sages have taught, all of the Jewish people comprise one integral organism.

Another point and principle, expressing double consolation, is that just as G-d will most certainly rebuild the ruins of Zion and Jerusalem and gather the dispersed of Israel from the ends of the earth through our righteous <u>Moshiach</u>, so will He, without a doubt, remove the grief of the individual, fulfilling the promise embodied by the verse, "Awaken and sing, you who repose in the dust."[214]

Great will be the joy, the true joy, when all will be re-joined at the time of the resurrection of the dead.

There is yet a third point: In regard to Zion and Jerusalem, the Romans—and before them, the Babylonians—were given dominion only over the wood and stone, silver and gold of the Temple's physical manifestation but not over its inner spiritual essence that is contained within the heart of each and every Jew—for the nations have no dominion over this, and it stands eternally. So too, regarding the mourning of the individual, death dominates only the physical body and concerns of the deceased person. The soul, however, is eternal; it has merely ascended to the World of Truth. That is why any good deed [performed by the mourner] that accords with the will of the Giver of life, G-d, blessed be He, adds to the soul's delight and merit and to its general good.

May it be G-d's will that henceforth you and your family should know no hurt and pain and that in your actions in defense of our Holy Land, "the land which G-d's eyes are upon from the beginning of the year to the end of the year,"[215] and in your observance of the mitzvah of *tefillin*—and one mitzvah brings another in its wake—you will find comfort.

With esteem and blessing.

By the Grace of G-d
25th of Elul, 5738 [September 27, 1978]
Brooklyn, NY

The Family Zippel

Milan, Italy

Greeting and Blessing:

In these days of *Selichos* and *Rachamim*, which bring the outgoing year to its end and prepare for the new year, I am addressing these lines to you, hoping they will bring you some comfort.

To begin with, there are many matters and occurrences that are hard for the human mind to understand. Among them also such that even if they can be understood intellectually, they are hard to accept emotionally. Specifically, in a case of bereavement.

Nevertheless, every Jew has been instructed by the Creator and Master of the world that the matters connected with *avelus* (mourning) must be limited in time, though during the proper time it is natural and proper to give vent to one's pain and sorrow at the sad loss, in keeping with the nature which G-d implanted in man.

However, when the various periods of mourning pass—the first three days profound grief and tears, the seven days of *shivah*, *sheloshim*, etc.—then it is not permitted to extend these periods beyond their allotted days. And since this is the instruction of the Creator and Master of the world, it is clear that carrying out these Divine instructions is within the capability of every Jew, for G-d does not expect the impossible of His creatures, and provides everyone beforehand with the necessary capacity and strength to carry out its instructions as set forth in His Torah, called *Toras Emes*, because it is true and realistic in all its teachings and imperatives.

It follows also that those who think that the gradual lessening of mourning, as above, may cause the soul of the departed that is now in the World of Truth to feel slighted are totally wrong, for the opposite is true. Indeed, excessive mourning by relatives is not good for the soul in the World of Truth, seeing that it is instrumental in this improper conduct on the part of its relatives here on earth; improper—because it is not in keeping with the spirit and letter of the Torah.

Undoubtedly, there is also a rational explanation for the above. One explanation, as mentioned at length on another occasion, is that the soul is, of course, eternal, as is universally recognized. It would be contrary even to logic and common sense to think that a physical disorder to the body could effect the vitality and existence of the soul, which is a purely spiritual being. The only thing that a sickness or fatal accident can do is to cause a weakening or termination of the bond that holds the body and soul together, whereupon the soul departs from its temporary abode in this world and returns to its original world of pure spirit in the eternal world.

Needless to say, insofar as the soul is concerned, it is a *release* from its "imprisonment" in the body. For, so long as it is bound up with the body, it suffers from physical limitations of the body, which necessarily constrain the soul and involve it in physical activities which are essentially alien to its purely spiritual nature. Nevertheless, the departure and ascent of the soul to its Heavenly abode is mourned for a time by the surviving relatives and friends, because the person is no longer *physically* here on earth and can no longer be seen and heard and felt by the physical senses and is therefore sadly missed. However, the soul itself retains all its faculties and, as explained in our holy sources, reacts to the conduct and feelings of its relatives left behind, sharing in their joys and in their sorrows and benefiting from their good deeds, especially those done on behalf of the soul, and it prays and intercedes on behalf of its relatives here on earth.

In other words, the departure of the soul from the body is a great advantage and ascent for the soul, and the loss is only for the bereaved, and to that extent it is also painful for the soul, of course.

There is yet another point that causes pain to the soul after departing from the body. While the soul is "clothed" in the body, it can actively participate with the body in all matters of Torah and *Mitzvot* and good deeds practiced in the daily life here on earth. But since all this involves physical action and tangible objects, the soul can no longer engage in these activities when it returns to its Heavenly abode, where it can only enjoy the fruits of the Torah and *Mitzvot* and good deeds performed by it in its sojourn on earth. Henceforth, the soul must depend on its relatives and friends to do *mitzvot* and good deeds also on its behalf, and this is the source of true gratification for the soul and helps it ascend to even greater heights.

In summary, it is not surprising that the human intellect cannot grasp the ways of G-d and why He should take away good persons who practiced good deeds all their life and helped spread G-dliness on earth through spreading the Torah and *Mitzvot*, which they would have continued to do had they been spared more years. It is not surprising, because a human being is a created thing and limited in all his aspects, and no creature can possibly understand the Creator. By way of simple illustration: An infant cannot understand the wisdom of a very wise man or scientist, although the scientist was himself an infant at one time, and the present infant could in time become an even greater scientist than the other. If, therefore, this is not surprising even though the difference and distance between the infant and the scientist is only relative, how much less surprising is it, where the difference is absolute and quite incomparable, as between a created being and the Creator.

Secondly, knowing that G-d is the Essence of goodness

and benevolence, and "it is in the nature of the Benevolent to do good," and "G-d is just and equitable," etc., which knowledge is one of the very basic tenets of our Faith, as explained at length in the Written Torah and Oral Torah—it is certain that all that G-d does is for the good.

Thirdly, it is also certain that the *Neshama* in *Olam HoEmes* waits and expects that all the good deeds it had been doing while here on earth, and would have continued doing had G-d given her more years in this world, would be continued on its behalf by all near and dear ones. Certainly it expects that the mourning periods will not be extended beyond the prescribed time, since this would be contrary to the teaching of the Torah.

Moreover, when it concerns persons who were brought up, and who brought up their children, in the way of the Torah, which is called *Toras Chesed*, a Torah of Lovingkindness, whose Golden Rule is *V'Ohavto L'Reacho Komocho*, making it the privilege and duty of every Jew to spread the Torah and *Mitzvot* to the utmost of their capability and to do all things of Torah and *Mitzvot* with joy and gladness of heart and who themselves personified all these qualities—all that has been said above is underscored with even greater emphasis.

Much more could be said on the subjects mentioned in this letter, but I am sure that the above will suffice, in keeping with the saying, "Give instruction to the wise person, and he will increase his wisdom still more" (Proverbs 9:9).

May G-d bless each and all of you, in the midst of all our people, that henceforth only goodness and benevolence be with you always and inscribe and seal you all for a good and sweet year in the good that is revealed and obvious.

With esteem and blessing,

M. Schneerson

P.S. It is a timely, meaningful, and everlasting memorial to the souls of the dear departed that the holy book of Tanya was published these days in Milan and dedicated to them. May their souls be bound up in the bond of eternal life.

By the Grace of G-d
14 Teves, 5730 [December 23, 1969]
Brooklyn, NY

Blessing and Greeting!

I received, on time, your letter—though circumstances have delayed my answer—in which you write of the passing of your mother, OBM, and your thoughts and feelings in connection with this.

The truth is that "none among us knows anything at all" concerning the ways of G-d, Who created humans, directs them and observes them with a most specific Divine Providence. But certainly, certainly, He is the very essence of good, and, as the expression goes, "it is in the nature of the good to do good." If, at times, what G-d does is at all not understood by the human mind— little wonder: what significance has a limited, measured, finite creature in relation to the infinite and endless and especially in relation to "the absolutely Infinite and Endless" *(beli gevul ve-ein sof ha-amiti)*?

Nevertheless, G-d chose to reveal a fraction of His wisdom to man, to flesh and blood. This He did with His holy Torah, called "the Torah of light" and "the Torah of life"—that is to say, it illuminates man's path in life in such a manner that even his limited faculties may comprehend its light. Thus, also in the case of this occurrence and similar ones, one can find an understanding—at least a partial one—in accordance with what is explained in our (Written and Oral) Torah.

Actually, this understanding is to be found in two rulings of Torah law which address our actual conduct in these circumstances. At first glance, they seem to stand in contradiction one to the other, though they appear in the same section of the Code of Jewish Law. The section (*Yoreh Deah* 394) begins: "One must not mourn excessively (beyond what our Sages have instructed us); one who does so in extreme…." Yet at the section's end, it is brought that "one who does not mourn as the Sages have guided us is a callous and cruel person." Now, if in such a case it is natural to mourn, what's so terrible about one who mourns more? Why the harsh rebuke mentioned in the law? And if to mourn excessively is so terrible, why is it cruel to mourn less?

The explanation lies in the concluding words of our Sages (as quoted from Maimonides): "One should fear and worry, search one's deeds and repent."

It is self-understood that the soul is eternal. Obviously, an illness of the flesh or blood cannot terminate or diminish the life of the soul—it can only damage the flesh and the blood themselves and the bond between them and the soul, that is to say, it can bring to the cessation of this bond—death, G-d forbid. And with the severing of what binds the soul to the flesh, the soul ascends and frees herself of the shackles of the body, of its limitations and restrictions. Through the good deeds she has performed during the period she was upon earth and within the body, she is elevated to a higher, much higher, level than her status prior to her descent into the body. As our Sages expressed it: The descent of the soul is a descent for the sake of an ascent, an ascent above and beyond her prior state.

From this it is understood that anyone close to this soul, anyone to whom she was dear, must appreciate that the soul has ascended, higher even than the level she was at previously; it is only that in our lives, in our world, it is a loss. And just as the closer one is to the soul, all the more precious to them is the soul's elevation, so it is with the second aspect—the intensity of the pain. For they, all the more so, feel the loss of her departure from the body and from life in this world.

Also, it is a loss in the sense that—it seems—the soul could have ascended even higher by remaining in this world, as our Sages taught in *Ethics of Our Fathers*: "One moment of repentance and good deeds in this world is preferable to the entire World to Come."

Thus, since the occurrence contains these two conflicting facets—on the one hand, the freeing of the soul from the body's shackles and her ascent to a higher world, the World of Truth; on the other, the abovementioned loss—the result is the two rulings. The "Torah of Truth" mandates that one mourn for the time period set by our Sages. At the same time, it is forbidden to mourn excessively (that is, beyond the set mourning period, and also in regards to the intensity of the mourning within these days).

As said, the primary cause for mourning such an occurrence is the loss on the part of the living. This is the object of the mourning period: The living need to understand why it is that they deserved this loss. This is why "one should fear and worry, search one's deeds and repent."

Through this, another thing is attained—the endurance of the bond between the living and the soul who has ascended. For the soul is enduring and eternal and sees and observes what is taking place with those connected with her and close to her. Every good deed they do causes her spiritual pleasure—specifically, the accomplishments of those she has educated and raised with the education that brings the said good deeds. That is to say, she has a part in those deeds resulting from the education she provided her children and the ones she influenced.

Since all of the above constitute directives of our Torah, the wisdom and will of G-d, the fulfillment of these directives is part and parcel of our service of G-d, of which it is said, "Serve G-d with joy." A directive of Torah also serves as the source of strength which provides the abilities to carry it out. Consequently, since the Torah addresses these instructions to each and every individual, it is within the capacity of each individual to carry it out—and, more so, to carry it out in a manner of "Serve G-d with joy."

All this applies to the entire family, but even more so, and with yet a greater supply of fortitude—as well as a greater degree of responsibility—in regard to those who are in a position to affect the other family members who will emulate their example. Therefore, the responsibility to implement all of the above falls first and foremost upon the head of the family and the senior child; in this case, I am referring to you and your father. The guarantee "If you have toiled, you will find" applies here as well.

In all the above also lies the answer to your question as to how you can lighten the load, etc.—through a behavior consistent with the above verse with a strong faith in G-d that you will succeed in this endeavor.

May it be the will of G-d that you have good tidings concerning all the above with open and revealed good.

With blessings for success in all your endeavors and good tidings,

[Signature: M. Schneerson]

Letter to a child of Holocaust survivors, who felt trapped by the questions and doubts raised by the Holocaust.

By the Grace of G-d
23 Shevat, 5744 [January 28, 1984]
Brooklyn, NY

Greeting and Blessing!

This is in reply to your letter of January 23, 1984, in which you write that you were born in a DP camp in Germany, a child of parents who survived the Holocaust, and you ask why G-d permitted the Holocaust to take place, etc. No doubt you know that there is substantial literature dealing with this terrible tragedy, and a letter is hardly the medium to deal adequately with the question. However, since you have written to me, I must give you an answer, hence, the following thoughts.

Jews—including you and me—are "believers, the children of believers," our Sages declare. Deep in one's heart, every Jew believes there is a G-d Who is the Creator and Master of the world and that the world has a purpose. Any thinking person who contemplates the solar system, for example, or the complexities of an atom, must come to the conclusion and conviction that our universe did not come about by some "freak accident." Wherever you turn, you see design and purpose.

It follows that a human being "also" has a purpose, certainly where millions of human beings are concerned. Since the Creator created the world with a purpose, it is also logical to assume that He wished the purpose to be realized and therefore would reveal to the only "creature" on earth who has an intelligence to understand such matters, namely, humankind, what this purpose is and how to go about realizing it. This, indeed, is the ultimate purpose of every human being, namely, to do his or her share in the realization of the Divine design and purpose of Creation. It is also common sense that without such "Divine revelation," a human being would not, of his own accord, know what exactly is that purpose and how to achieve it any more than a minuscule part or component in a highly complex system could comprehend the whole system, much less the creator of the system.

The illustration often given in this connection is the case of an infant, whose lack of ability to understand an intricate theory of a mature scientist would not surprise anyone, although both the infant and the scientist are created beings, and the difference between them is only relative, in terms of age and knowledge, etc. Indeed, it is possible that the infant may someday surpass the scientist in knowledge and insight. Should it, then, be surprising that a created human being cannot understand the ways of the Creator?

It is also understandable that since every person has a

G-d-given purpose in life, he or she is provided with the capacity to carry out that purpose fully.

A further important point to remember is that since G-d created everything with a purpose, there is nothing lacking or superfluous in the world. This includes also the human capacity. It follows that a person's capacity in terms of knowledge, time, energy, etc., must fully be applied to carrying out his, or her, purpose in life. If any of these resources is diverted to something that is extraneous to carrying out the Divine purpose, it would not only be misused and wasteful, but would detract to that extent from the real purpose.

In the Torah, called *Toras Chaim* ("instruction of living"), G-d has revealed what the purpose of Creation is and provided all the knowledge necessary for a human being, particularly a Jew, to carry it out in life. Having designated the Jewish people as a "kingdom of *Kohanim* [priests] and a holy nation," a Jew is required to live up to all the Divine precepts in the Torah. Gentiles are required to keep only the Seven Basic Moral Laws, the so-called Seven Noahide Laws, with all their ramifications—which must be the basis of any and every human society, if it is to be human in accordance with the will and design of the Creator.

One of the basic elements of the Divine design, as revealed in the Torah, is that G-d desires it to be carried out by choice and not out of compulsion. Every human being has, therefore, the free will to live in accordance with G-d's Will or in defiance of it.

With all the above in mind, let us return to your question, which is one that has been on the minds of many: Why did G-d permit the Holocaust? The only answer we can give is: only G-d knows.

However, [the very fact that there is no answer to this question is, in itself, proof that one is not required to know the answer, or understand it, *in order to fulfill one's purpose in life*.] Despite the lack of satisfactory answer to the awesome and tremendous "Why?"—one can, and must, carry on a meaningful and productive life, promote justice and kindness in one's surroundings, and indeed, help create a world where there should be no room for any holocaust or for any kind of man's inhumanity to man.

As a matter of fact, in the above there is an answer to an unspoken question: "What should my reaction be?" The answer to this question is certain: It must be seen as a challenge to every Jew—because Jews were the principal victims of the Holocaust—a challenge that should be met head-on, with all resolve and determination, namely, that regardless of how long it will take the world to repent for the Holocaust and make the world a fitting place to live in for all human beings—I, for one, will not slacken in my determination to carry out my purpose in life, which is to serve G-d, wholeheartedly and with joy, and make this world a fitting abode—not only for humans, but also for the *Shechinah*, the Divine Presence itself.

Of course, much more could be said on the subject, but why dwell on such a painful matter when there is so much good to be done?

With blessing.

[P.S. Needless to say, the above may be accepted intellectually, and it may ease the mind, but it cannot assuage the pain and upheaval, especially of one who has been directly victimized by the Holocaust. Thus, in this day and age of rampant suspicion, etc., especially when one is not known personally, one may perhaps say—"Well, it is easy for one who is not emotionally involved to give an 'intellectual' explanation...."

So, I ought, perhaps, to add that I, too, lost in the Holocaust very close and dear relatives such as a grandmother, brother, cousins, and others (G-d should avenge their blood). But life according to G-d's command must go on, and the sign of life is in growth and creativity.]

By the Grace of G-d
3rd of Nissan, 5738 [April 10, 1978]
Brooklyn, NY

Greeting and Blessing:

I am in receipt of your letter, in which you write about happenings in the family and ask why such untoward happenings did occur, though you find nothing in your conduct and activities that would justify them.

I surely do not have to point out to you that the question of "why do the righteous suffer and the wicked prosper?" is a very old one and was already asked by *Moshe Rabbeinu*, who received the Torah from G-d and handed it over to each and every Jew as an everlasting inheritance for all times. As you probably also know, the whole book of *Iyov* (Job) is devoted to this problem, and it has been dealt with ever since.

The point of the answer given by our Sages, as it has often been explained at length, is by way of the example of a small child who does not understand why his father, who is such a wise and kind person, sometimes acts in a way which causes a child pain and tears. It would not surprise any person that the child is not in a position to understand the ways of his father, although, be it noted, only a number of years separate them in age and also in intelligence. At the same time, the child instinctively feels and knows that his father loves him, and surely everything is for his benefit and not for the benefit of any other child or for his own benefit, since it would be unthinkable that a father who has a one and only son would cause pain to his child for the benefit of a stranger or for his own benefit.

If this is so in the case of a child and his father, where the distinction between them is only relative in terms of age and intelligence, as mentioned above, how much more so in the case of a created being and the Creator, where the distinction is absolute and unbridgeable. Indeed, it would have been most surprising if a human being could understand the way of G-d except to the extent that G-d Himself, in His kindness, has revealed some aspects of His Divine Providence and in a necessarily very limited way. Moreover, our Torah, *Toras Chayim* and *Toras Emes*, assures us that when a Jew strengthens his *bitochon* and trust in G-d, Whose benevolent Divine Providence extends to each and every one individually and Who is the essence of goodness, and it is the nature of the good to do good—this in itself opens new insights into a better understanding of G-d's ways and at the same time speeds G-d's blessings in the kind of good that is revealed and evident.

And, as mentioned earlier, this fact that *Moshe Rabbeinu* already pondered this question did not in the least affect his simple faith in G-d and did not in any way affect his observance of the Torah and *mitzvot* in his daily life and conduct, and this is also what he bequeathed to each and every Jew in all future generations.

It is surely also unnecessary to point out that this question that might arise under certain circumstances in the life of an individual can just as well be asked in connection with the long-suffering history of our people in exile for the past 1,900 years and more. Yet here, too, despite the persecutions, martyrdom, and suffering, our people tenaciously clung to the Torah and *mitzvot* as their only way of life, and it has not weakened their belief in and confident hope of the ultimate true and complete *geula* through our righteous Moshiach, when it will become apparent that the whole long and dark exile was a blessing in disguise.

Much more could be said in this subject, but I hope that the above will suffice to help you regain fully your true Jewish perspective, especially as what has been written above is not intended to answer the question once and for all but merely to help minimize the doubts and questions which might distract a Jew from his innate, simple faith in G-d and in His infinite lovingkindness and justice, which is an integral part of every Jew's heritage.

At this time before Pesach, the festival of our liberation, I send you and yours prayerful wishes for a kosher and inspiring Pesach and a fuller measure of liberation from all distractions so as to be able to serve G-d wholeheartedly and with joy.

With blessing.

A letter related to *mezuzah*:

By the Grace of G-d
Rosh Chodesh Elul, 5736 [August 27, 1976]
Brooklyn, NY

To the Jewish mothers and daughters everywhere,
G-d bless you—

Blessing and Greeting:

In view of the recent events—the hijacking and saving
of the hostages held in Uganda and the subsequent
attempt of the terrorists to perpetrate a vicious reprisal,
G-d forbid, in Kushta (Istanbul):

It should be understood that these events are an indica-
tion that Jews must, at the earliest possible, strengthen
all aspects of their security and defenses—first and
foremost in their spiritual life, which is the channel
to receive G-d's blessings also in the physical aspect,
namely, to know the right ways and means that have to
be undertaken in the natural order of things and to fully
succeed in these efforts, in accordance with the Divine
promise, "G-d, your G-d, will bless you in all that you
do"—to be protected and secured from enemies and to
be spared any undesirable happenings, G-d forbid.

The above events remind each and all of our Jewish
brethren in general and Jewish mothers and daughters

in particular—since every married Jewish woman is called *akeres habayis*, "foundation of the home," and those not yet married are to be *akeres habayis*, for which they must prepare themselves from tender age—the following:

The present situation calls for the protection of every Jewish home. True protection is that which only G-d provides, as it is written, "G-d guards the city." To ensure this Divine guardianship, the home has to be conducted in all aspects according to G-d's will.

Then the home is also an abode for the *Shechinah* (G-d's Presence), in accordance with His promise, "I will dwell among them."

In addition to this, G-d has given our people a special gift wherewith to protect the home, namely, the mitzvah of *mezuzah*. Our Sages declare explicitly that "the home is protected by it (the *mezuzah*)."

Moreover, this protection embraces the members of the household also when they go out of the house, as it is written, 'G-d will guard your going and your coming from now and forever.' It is further explained in our holy sources that the Divine Name (*Shin-Dalet-Yud*) written on the back of the sacred *mezuzah* parchment spells out the words, "*Shomer Dalsos Yisroel*—Guardian of Jewish Doors."

Let it also be remembered that inasmuch as all Jews constitute one body and are bound up with one another, every *mezuzah* is a Divine protection not only for the individual home, with everybody and everything in it, but each additional kosher *mezuzah* that is affixed on a doorpost of any Jewish home, anywhere, adds to the protection of all our people everywhere.

And considering—as mentioned above—that every Jewish housewife is an *akeres habayis*, and every Jewish girl a future *akeres habayis*, they have a special *zechus* (merit) and responsibility in the matter of *mezuzah* to see to it that not only a kosher *mezuzah* be affixed on every doorpost in their home that is required to have a *mezuzah* but that the same be done by their Jewish neighbors and friends and in all Jewish homes.

I hope and pray that you will do this with inspiration and joy, which, in addition to increasing the *hatzlocho* [success] in this effort, will also inspire many others to do likewise, and the *zechus horabim* [the merit you brought to the many] will further stand you in good stead.

The present time is particularly auspicious for this endeavor, as for endeavors in all matters of goodness and holiness, since we are in the beginning of the month of *Elul*—the month of spiritual stock-taking, to complete the deficiencies of the outgoing year and to prepare for the New Year, that it be a good and blessed year for each and all of us and for our Jewish people as a whole.

With esteem and blessing of *kesivo vechasimo tovah*,

[M. Schneerson]

ENDNOTES

1. *Bereishit Rabbah* 51:3; *Iggeret Hakodesh*, 11.
2. *Likkutei Torah, Nitzavim* 44a; based on Jerusalem Talmud, *Nedarim* 9:4 and *Taamei HaMitzvot, Kedoshim*.
3. *Igrot Kodesh*, vol. 25, pp. 3-5. *Torat Menachem—Menachem Tzion*, vol. 2, pp. 536-537. A translation of the full text of the Rebbe's letter to Ariel Sharon, which also includes a number of the other themes the Rebbe evoked on in his responses to those who have suffered a tragedy, is presented on page 189. We will be citing additional passages from this letter in later chapters.
4. See Maimonides' Thirteen Principles, enumerated in his commentary on the Mishnah, introduction to *Sanhedrin*, chapter 11.
5. Isaiah 26:19.
6. From a letter by the Rebbe dated 25th of Elul, 5738 [September 27, 1978]. See above, p. 193, for the full text of the letter.
7. *Sichot Kodesh 5733*, vol. 2, pp. 30-32. A video recording of the Rebbe's talk, courtesy of JEM, can be accessed at: www.chabad.org/1491002.
8. See *Torat Menachem—Hitvaaduyot 5720*, vol. 1, p. 396.
9. This is quoted from a personal letter the Rebbe sent to Mrs. Sharfstein, dated 29th of Sivan, 5718 [June 17, 1958]. The entire letter can be found in her book, *Beyond the Dollar Line*, pages 240-241.
10. Ibid.

11. From a letter by the Rebbe dated 5th of Tammuz, 5743 [June 16, 1983]. For the full text of the letter, see: www.chabad.org/1852670.

12. Psalms 31:19.

13. Adapted from Maimonides, Introduction to *Sanhedrin*, chapter 11. See also Maimonides, Laws of *Teshuvah*, ch. 8.

14. *Torat Menachem—Menachem Tzion*, vol. 2, p. 558.

15. *To Know and to Care* (Sichos in English), vol. 2, ch. 14.

16. *Igrot Kodesh*, vol. 26, p. 271. *Torat Menachem—Menachem Tzion*, vol. 2, p. 543. See p. 199 for the full text of the letter.

17. *Avot* 4:17.

18. *Igrot Kodesh*, vol. 25, p. 5. *Torat Menachem—Menachem Tzion*, vol. 2, p. 537.

19. From a letter by the Rebbe dated 25th of Elul, 5738 [September 27, 1978]. See above, p. 193, for the full text of the letter.

20. *Torat Menachem—Hitvaaduyot 5742*, vol. 4, pp. 2013-2014.

21. The full story of the terror attack and the Rebbe's response to it can be seen below in chapters 12 and 14.

22. *Igrot Kodesh*, vol. 13, p. 167. *Torat Menachem—Menachem Tzion*, vol. 2, p. 503.

23. See *Igrot Kodesh*, vol. 25, p. 46. *Torat Menachem—Menachem Tzion*, vol. 2, p. 540.

24. From a letter by the Rebbe dated 5th of Tammuz, 5743 [June 16, 1983]. For the full text of the letter, see: www.chabad.org/1852670.

25. From a letter by the Rebbe dated September 27, 1978. See p. 193 for the full text of the letter.

26. Ibid.

27. Ibid. As noted in the previous chapter, the actions of those who are grieving affect the soul of the deceased. Grieving that is prolonged beyond what the Torah pre-

scribes would therefore cause pain to the departed soul as well.

In a separate letter written to the daughter of a young woman who had suddenly passed away (*Igrot Kodesh*, vol. 26, p. 271; *Torat Menachem—Menachem Tzion*, vol. 2, p. 543). The Rebbe writes: "All this applies to the entire family, but even more so, and with yet a greater supply of fortitude—as well as a greater degree of responsibility—in regard to those who are in a position to affect the other family members who will emulate their example. Therefore, the responsibility to implement all of the above falls first and foremost upon the head of the family and the senior child. In this case, I am referring to you and your father. The guarantee, 'You have toiled, you have found,' applies here as well."

28. From a letter by the Rebbe dated 5th of Tammuz, 5743 [June 16, 1983]. For the full text of the letter, see: www.chabad.org/1852670.

29. Rabbi Raphael Grossman, *My Encounter with the Rebbe Interview*, January 30, 2012.

30. Mr. Naftali Deutsch, *My Encounter with the Rebbe Interview*, September 11, 2011.

31. *Sefer Hasichot 5748*, vol. 1, pp. 310-311. A recording of this talk, courtesy of JEM, can be heard at www.chabad. org/554612.

32. From an interview with Mr. Schiffman by the *My Encounter* project. The interview, which was conducted by JEM, can be accessed at: www.chabad.org/2258149.

33. *Avodah Zarah* 3a.

34. Told by Rabbi Shabtai Slavaticki.

35. See for example *Igrot Kodesh*, vol. 22, p. 356.

36. *Sichot Kodesh 5736*, vol. 2, p. 633ff.

37. *Igrot Kodesh*, vol. 25, p. 46. *Torat Menachem—Menachem Tzion*, vol. 2, p. 540. In conjunction with the Rebbe's request, Shifra Morozov, a follower of the

Rebbe, whose husband David, an Israeli soldier, had been killed in the Six-Day War, began arranging bar mitzvah celebrations under Chabad auspices for the orphans of Israeli heroes. Each year since, as many as four thousand people have gathered in Kfar Chabad, where a special celebration takes place for the tens of orphans turning thirteen that year. The Rebbe would send each young man a personal letter offering his own best wishes and a pair of *tefillin*.

38. From a letter by the Rebbe dated 25th of Elul, 5738 [September 27, 1978]. See above, p. 193, for the full text of the letter.

39. *Igrot Kodesh*, vol. 15, p. 303. *Torat Menachem—Menachem Tzion*, vol. 2, p. 505.

40. Told by Rabbi Moshe Feller.

41. Told by a grandchild.

42. Told by Dr. Feldman's daughter, Mrs. Sara Shemtov.

43. *Torat Menachem—Menachem Tzion*, vol. 2, p. 566.

44. Genesis 23:1.

45. See Rashi's commentary on Genesis 23:2.

46. The Rebbe is perhaps alluding to the verse in Psalms (90:10): "The days of our lives number seventy years, and if in great vigor, eighty years."

47. *Torat Menachem—Menachem Tzion*, vol. 2, p. 568.

48. *Otzar Sippurei Chabad*, vol. 1, p. 93ff. For an English version, see "The Reincarnated Prince" by Tuvia Bolton: www.chabad.org/421892.

49. As told by Rabbi Michoel Seligson.

50. *Avot d'Rabbi Natan*, chapter 14.

51. *Midrash Mishlei* 31.

52. *Why? Reflections on the Loss of a Loved One*, p. 38.

53. Ibid., p. 42.

54. *Igrot Kodesh*, vol. 17, p. 273.

55. *Sichot Kodesh 5752*, vol. 2, pp. 649-650.

56. Mrs. Sara Labkowski, *My Encounter with the Rebbe Interview*, October 7, 2014.

57. See also *Sichot Kodesh 5730*, vol. 1, p. 662.

58. When the survivors of Glubokoye wanted to create a museum in Israel to honor the memory of their beloved community, which was decimated during the Holocaust, the Rebbe urged them to invest instead in educating the present and future generations:
What benefit will come to these departed souls, of righteous memory, by adding yet another museum in the Holy Land.... With the sum of money you write of, which you are willing to invest in the building, you can educate hundreds of descendants of Glubokoye in their heritage! (translation of the Rebbe's reply [in archives of the Chabad library]).

59. *Igrot Kodesh*, vol. 6, pp. 175-176.

60. From a letter dated 23th of Shevat, 5744 [January 28, 1984]. See above, p. 204, for the full text of the letter.

61. See *Sefer Hasichot 5748*, vol. 1, pp. 272-274.

62. *Igrot Kodesh*, vol. 30, p. 92.

63. At a special gathering, which took place on Saturday night during the *shivah* of Rabbi Dovid Okunov, a resident of Crown Heights who was fatally shot while on his way to prayers, the Rebbe spoke of the horrific loss: "...from time to time there occur events that are completely and utterly incomprehensible...when we experience a [moment] of unparalleled darkness...[in this instance, the murder of a righteous individual] on his way to do a mitzvah...." While speaking, the Rebbe broke down and cried, and hundreds of Chasidim also wept. But the Rebbe composed himself and announced that a yeshiva would be built "to bestow honor at his death," a Talmudic reference to the Torah academy established by the Kingdom of Judah and the inhabitants of Jerusalem as a means to "bestow honor upon Hezeki-

ah at his death." The Rebbe suggested that since, at the
time of his murder, R. Dovid was working to help Jews
who were trapped behind the Iron Curtain, it would be
fitting that a Jewish day school be dedicated in his hon-
or to serving the needs of boys from the Soviet Union.

64. *Igrot Kodesh*, vol. 19, pp. 209-210.

65. *Torat Menachem—Hitvaaduyot 5720*, vol. 1, pp. 466-
468.

66. Maimonides, Laws of Mourning, end of chapter 13.

67. Dated 1ˢᵗ Day of Chanukah, 5730 [December 5, 1969].
For the full text of the letter, see:
www.chabad.org/266343.

68. See *Seeds of Wisdom*, p. 52, published by JEM.

69. *Avot* 4:17.

70. Simon Jacobson, *Toward a Meaningful Life*, p. 83 (William Morrow, Harper Collins, 1995).

71. *Igrot Kodesh*, vol. 13, p. 30.

72. Ibid., pp. 36-37. *Torat Menachem—Menachem Tzion*,
vol. 2, pp. 496-497.

73. In his commentary to Genesis 37:35.

74. Genesis 37:34-35.

75. Ibid. 38:14.

76. Avraham Maisha Deitch, *My Encounter with the Rebbe
Interview*, April 1, 2012.

77. Rabbi Raphael Grossman, *My Encounter with the Rebbe
Interview*, January 30, 2012.

78. Genesis, chapter 40.

79. See the commentary of Rabbi Samson Raphael Hirsh,
ad loc.

80. In the summer of 1990, after a series of tragic car acci-
dents that took the lives of some of the members of the
Lubavitch community in Melbourne, Australia, Rabbi
Leibel Groner, one of the Rebbe's secretaries, wrote a
note to the Rebbe expressing his fears and concerns over
the fact that so many lives had been lost in so short a

time. The Rebbe responded: "It is high time to fulfill the directive of our Rebbes 'Think positive, and it will be positive' in a literal way!"

81. *Berachot* 56a-b.

82. Based on this teaching, the *Zohar* (I:183a) says that one should tell dreams to friends, not enemies, and brings proof from Joseph of the Bible who told his brothers his dreams, but since they disliked him and had negative thoughts about the dream's fruition, it took twenty-two years for the dream to materialize. Based on this Talmudic passage, Abarbanel explains that Joseph actually recounted his dreams to his brothers in order to allow them to interpret the dreams according to their liking. He did this in order to allay their jealousy of him and prove his loyalty and love for them.

83. Ibid. 60a.

84. Ibid.

85. On Shabbat *Parashat Beshalach*. The Rebbe revisited this theme during an address he gave on Shabbat *Parashat Shemot*, 1966. See *Likkutei Sichot*, vol. 36, p. 1ff for the published version of both of these talks.

86. After all, according to scripture (Ecclesiastes 7:20): "There is no righteous man upon this earth that does (only) good and never fails." Indeed, the Midrash (*Bereishit Rabbah* 76:1), according to the interpretation of various commentaries (specifically *Be'or Hasechel* and *Nezer Kodesh*), points out that Jacob, the greatest among the Patriarchs, and Moses, the greatest among the Prophets, both experienced fear on occasion precisely as a result of their concern that perhaps they were undeserving of Divine salvation!

87. Traditional Judaism believes that all of the so-called punishments outlined in the Torah serve not to harm the one being punished but to cleanse them of the spiritual blemish caused by sin and are thus not aimed

at hurting but rather healing, not unlike the notion of disciplinary acts called "tough love," which we sometimes need to administer to those we love for their betterment.

88. In fact, according to Nachmanides (Leviticus 26:11): "When the majority of the Jewish people are complete [in their faith in G-d], their affairs are not run by the natural order…to the extent that there is no need for a physician or to follow the ways of medicine, as it says, 'I am the L-rd your healer….'" Obviously, those times of spiritual perfection are all too rare, and under the current circumstances, we are encouraged to follow the natural order of things.

89. Also see chapter 20 below, "Optimism in the Face of Tragedy."

90. *Igrot Kodesh*, vol. 3, p. 373.

91. *Igrot Kodesh*, vol. 4, p. 198.

92. Based on the principle that verbalizing negativity can bring about negativity, the Rebbe once explained (see earlier footnote 62 for sources) the sequence of verses that describes Moses' second foray into public life: "He went out on the second day, and behold, two Hebrew men were quarreling, and he said to the wicked one, "Why are you going to strike your friend?" And he retorted [to Moses], "Who made you a man, a prince, and a judge over us? Do you plan to slay me as you have slain the Egyptian?" Moses became frightened and said, "Indeed, the matter has become known!" Pharaoh heard of this incident, and he sought to slay Moses, etc." The Rebbe explained that the Torah records not just Moses' fear but that he verbalized his fear (an irrelevant detail, it would seem): "he said, 'the matter has become known'" in order to teach that speaking aloud his fears were what brought him to "Pharaoh heard of this incident and sought to slay Moses."

93. Published in *Meah Shearim*, 28a-b. *Maamarei Admur Hazaken Haketzarim*, p. 446.

94. *Igrot kodesh*, vol. 6, pp. 286-287.

95. Here the Rebbe alluded to a point he often made to those who came to seek his blessing for good health, where he linked one's physical health to their spiritual well-being. See for example *Igrot Kodesh*, vol. 17, p. 242, where the Rebbe writes: "It is clear that a physical ailment needs to be treated by improving one's spiritual health as well. When one improves the vitality of the soul, this has the effect of improving the vitality of the body and aids in the effectiveness of the medical treatment...."

    The Rebbe advised doctors similarly: "I am sure that you follow the practice of many G-d-fearing doctors in advising patients who seek your advice regarding a health problem that it is appropriate to also effect a healing of the soul..." (See *Igrot Kodesh*, vol. 15, p. 150).

96. *Igrot Kodesh*, vol. 9, p. 281.

97. Heard from R. Zalman Gurary with whom the story took place.

98. See *Igrot Kodesh*, vol. 4, page 130.

99. This statement recalls a well-known line attributed to David Ben-Gurion who said, referring to Jewish history as a whole: "A Jew who doesn't believe in miracles is not a realist."

100. From a 5712 [1951-1952] letter by the Rebbe. For the full text of the letter, see: www.chabad.org/3006265.

101. On October 27, 1991, a man came to see the Rebbe for "Sunday dollars" with a friend who was ill. "This gentleman would like a blessing for a difficult operation he will be having tomorrow," he said to the Rebbe. "Why must you worry him by calling it a difficult surgery?" the Rebbe responded with a smile. "Call it an

easy surgery [instead]." Turning to the man who was ill, the Rebbe concluded: "The main thing is that you have a speedy recovery and an easy and healthy life."

102. From a letter by the Rebbe dated 3rd of Adar, 5737 [February 21, 1977].

103. *Igrot Kodesh*, vol. 4, p. 288.

104. *Seeds of Wisdom*, p. 98, published by JEM.

105. *Likkutei Sichot*, vol. 12, pp. 258-260.

106. *Igrot Kodesh*, vol. 13, p. 205.

107. Letter to Eliezer Steinman. *Igrot Kodesh*, vol. 13, pp. 239-241. *Torat Menachem—Menachem Tzion*, vol. 2, p. 504 (emphasis added). See chapter 28.

108. Maimonides, Laws of Mourning 13:9 and 13:3.

109. Mr. Avner, *My Encounter with the Rebbe Interview*, December 29, 2006.

110. As told by Mrs. Kozenn-Chajes.

111. Rabbi Yitzchak Vorst, *Why? Reflections on the Loss of a Loved One*, p. 41.

112. See chapter 11.

113. Dated 1st Day of Chanukah, 5730 [December 5, 1969]. A video of Rabbi Weiner telling this story, courtesy of JEM, is available on www.chabad.org/1130177.

114. An undated letter by the Rebbe.

115. *Megillah* 14a.

116. Deuteronomy 25:17.

117. *Avot* 4:21.

118. *Igrot Kodesh*, vol. 23, pp. 373-375. See also ibid., vol. 25, p. 56ff.

119. See http://lubavitch.com/news/article/2030937/ In-Conversation-with-Nobel-Prize-Winner-Elie-Wiesel. html.

120. When Eli and Marion's son, Elisha, was born, the Rebbe sent representatives to the *brit milah* (circumcision),

who brought them a note from the Rebbe in which he wrote that his heart and soul were overflowing with joy.

121. The following are some examples of Hitler's pronouncements that revealed the reasons behind his venomous hatred of the Jews: "The struggle for world domination will be fought entirely between us, between Germans and Jews. All else is facade and illusion. Behind England stands Israel, and behind France, and behind the United States. Even when we have driven the Jew out of Germany, he remains our world enemy." (Cited by Hermann Rauschning in *Hitler Speaks*, p. 234.) "If only one country, for whatever reason, tolerates a Jewish family in it, that family will become the germ center for fresh sedition. If one little Jewish boy survives without any Jewish education, with no synagogue and no Hebrew school, it [Judaism] is in his soul. Even if there had never been a synagogue or a Jewish school or an Old Testament, the Jewish spirit would still exist and exert its influence. It has been there from the beginning and there is no Jew, not a single one, who does not personify it." (From a conversation with Croatian Foreign Minister General Kvaternik, July 21, 1941, cited by Robert Wistrich, *Hitler's Apocalypse*, p. 122.)

122. From an informal interview session between a group of Young Leadership Cabinet members of the U.J.A. (United Jewish Appeal) and the Rebbe, Sunday evening, March 4, 1962. An English transcript can be accessed at: www.chabad.org/354698.

123. *Sichot Kodesh 5734*, vol. 2, p. 183. *Torat Menachem—Menachem Tzion*, vol. 2, p. 416.

124. *Igrot Kodesh*, vol. 16, p. 212. *Torat Menachem—Menachem Tzion*, vol. 2, p. 510.

125. See the following link for a video, courtesy of JEM, of this episode: www.chabad.org/629696.

126. *Igrot Kodesh*, vol. 13, p. 61. *Torat Menachem—Menachem Tzion*, vol. 2, p. 501.

127. *Igrot Kodesh*, vol. 13, pp. 155-156. *Torat Menachem—Menachem Tzion*, vol. 2, p. 502.

128. *Igrot Kodesh by the Tzemach Tzedek*, p. 159; p. 168 (Kehot, 2013).

129. *Igrot Kodesh by the Alter Rebbe*, p. 430 (Kehot, 2012).

130. The Rebbe quoted this letter when consoling a grieving family. See *Igrot Kodesh*, vol. 10, pp. 306-308. *Torat Menachem—Menachem Tzion*, vol. 2, pp. 491-493.

131. See *Sefer Hasichot 5748*, vol. 1, p. 332.

132. As told by Simon Jacobson, the son of Gershon Ber, of blessed memory.

133. As a background for the ideas discussed in this chapter, see chapter 13 above, "Think Good."

134. *Igrot Kodesh*, vol. 20, p. 41.

135. *Igrot Kodesh*, vol. 12, pp. 270-271.

136. *Igrot Kodesh*, vol. 4, p. 55.

137. Rabbi Yosef Yitzchak's discourse was published before Shabbat in order to be studied on that Shabbat.

138. *Sichot Kodesh 5732*, vol. 1, pp. 362-364.

139. Quoted in part in chapter 2.

140. *Sichot Kodesh 5733*, vol. 2. pp. 30-33.

141. *Sichot Kodesh 5736*, vol. 2, pp. 413-415. In the continuation of the address, the Rebbe looked at another reason for the mission's success: "When they landed at the airport, what made victory possible was their utter thwarting of practical conventions…. Ordinarily, Israel would engage in the standard diplomatic formalities, consulting with all our so-called allies around the world—including even those who are clearly not our allies—and only then announce that we have sufficient weapons and troops, that the Cabinet has approved, and that we're going through with a specific operation. But here, the victory was achieved by ignoring the cal-

culations of time, space, the opinion of 'allies,' and the instincts of those carrying out the mission…and they succeeded."

142. John Hinckley Jr.'s father was John Warnock Hinckley, the president of World Vision United States, and chairman and president of the Vanderbilt Energy Corporation.

143. *Sichot Kodesh 5741*, vol. 3, pp. 107-109. www.chabad.org/968186.

144. The Seven Noahide Laws prohibit: idolatry, blasphemy, incest and adultery, murder, theft, and cruelty to animals. It also commands its followers to implement orderly processes of justice.

145. From a letter by the Lubavticher Rebbe, dated Erev Shabbat Kodesh Bereishit, 5747 [October 31, 1986]. For the full text of the letter, see: www.chabad.org/2021482.

146. See www.chabad.org/61921. It should be noted that in this instance, the Rebbe departed dramatically from his usual vehement insistence (see chapters 27 and 28), that the Holocaust would never happen again, often quoting the verse, *lo takum paamaim tzara,* which means, "An evil such as this will never reoccur."

   The difference between this occasion and others, though, is clear. The context of the Rebbe's discussion and statement to Swados was not theological, as it was on those occasions when the Rebbe declared that G-d would never again allow such an attack against the Jewish people. In this instance, their discussion touched on history and human nature and the susceptibility of a society that lacks a supreme moral authority as its anchor.

147. Numbers 22:3-4, based on Rashi's interpretation.

148. Rashi on Numbers 21:34. According to the Midrash, Og was the one who told Avraham that his nephew Lot

had been captured, prompting Abraham to rescue Lot. Moses feared that in the merit of this good deed, Og would win the war against the Israelites.

149. *Likkutei Sichot*, vol. 8, pp. 148-149.

150. *Igrot Kodesh*, vol. 10, p. 195.

151. In a letter to Zalman Shazar, the Rebbe writes: "...the idea to send a delegation to Israel was reinforced recently to serve as a means of lifting the spirits of the residents of Kfar Chabad...and even though we are under extreme financial pressure currently, in the hope that our conversation bear fruit, I have personally laid out the money to fund the tickets for travel" (*Igrot Kodesh*, vol. 13, p. 284).

152. The Rebbe's talk is printed in *Likkutei Sichot*, vol. 12, pp. 258-259.

153. An interesting example of this can be seen at: www.chabad.org/2139965 (courtesy of JEM).

154. *Igrot Kodesh*, vol. 24, p. 332.

155. For example, *Yediot Acharonot, Maariv, Haaretz*, and *Davar* of May 25, 1967.

156. *Sichot Kodesh 5727*, vol. 2, pp. 111-113.

157. The previous account is based on, and quotes directly from, a passage of the informative chapter titled "Israel" in Joseph Telushkin's comprehensive biography on the Rebbe (Harper Collins, 2014).

158. See: http://www.chabad.org/2600738.

159. Simon Jacobson, *Toward a Meaningful Life*, p. 138 (William Morrow, Harper Collins, 1995).

160. See *Menachot* 35b.

161. Psalms 8:3.

162. See, at length, *Ot B'Sefer Torah*, p. 210ff. (*Vaad Liktivat Sefer HaTorah Shel Yaldei Yisrael* [Kfar Chabad, 2009].)

163. From a letter by the Lubavitcher Rebbe, dated Rosh Chodesh Elul, 5736 [August 27, 1976]. See above, p. 212, for the full text of the letter. Further, the Rebbe

makes the following points: "Moreover, this protection embraces the members of the household also when they go out of the house, as it is written, 'G-d will guard your going and your coming from now and forever....' Let it also be remembered that inasmuch as all Jews constitute one body and are bound up with one another, every *mezuzah* is a Divine protection not only for the individual home, with everybody and everything in it, but each additional kosher *mezuzah* that is affixed on a doorpost of any Jewish home, anywhere, adds to the protection of all our people everywhere.

164. *Sichot Kodesh 5734*, vol. 2, pp. 146-147.

165. See *Igrot Kodesh*, vol. 16, p. 1 and p. 7.

166. A few days later, the young man sadly passed away from his injuries.

167. *Parashat Balak*, 14th of Tammuz, 5747 (1987).

168. This theme was also expressed by the Rebbe during the mourning period for his wife, when he said: "At this time we need to increase in brotherly love, 'the great principle of the Torah,' which is also connected to the verse 'The living shall take to heart...,' suggesting that whenever life is lost, it is a time to increase in love for another (*Sefer Hasichot 5748*, vol. 1, pp. 254-255).

169. *Igrot Kodesh*, vol. 13, p. 46. *Torat Menachem—Menachem Tzion*, vol. 2, p. 499.

170. The children of Israel are the children of G-d, as it explicitly states in the Torah: "You are children of the L-rd your G-d" (Deuteronomy 14:1) and "My son, My first-born Israel" (Exodus 4:22). The Almighty loves them as the prophets proclaim, "I love you, says G-d" (Malachi 1:2 and Hosea 11:1). The Baal Shem Tov taught that the love of the Almighty to every one of Israel is greater than the love of elderly parents to an only child born to them in their later years. (*Keter Shem Tov*, *Hosafot*, section 133)

171. II Samuel 23:2.
172. *Shir HaShirim Rabbah* 1:6:1.
173. *Sefer Hasichot 5751*, vol. 1, pp. 226-234, quoted in *To Love a Fellow Jew* by Rabbi Nissan Dovid Dubov, ch. 9.
174. See the *Musaf* prayer of Yom Kippur.
175. *Menachos* 29b.
176. See the *Musaf* prayer of Yom Kippur.
177. Genesis 15:13.
178. *Shemot Rabbah* 5:22. "And Moses returned to G-d and he said, 'Why have You done evil to this people....' This is what Moses said to G-d: 'I took the Book of Genesis and I read it, and I saw the deeds of the generation of the flood and how they were judged, the generation of the Tower of Babel and how they were judged, but this nation, what did they do that they were sent into servitude—a decree greater than all the previous generations?'"
179. Isaiah 54:7.
180. See *Pesachim* 50a.
181. Exodus 34:6-7.
182. *Iggeret Hakodesh*, 22.
183. Jeremiah 10:19 and Psalms 91:15.
184. See *Sefer Hasichot 5750*, vol. 1, pp. 378-388.
185. Ibid.
186. When Rabbi Levi Yitzchak of Berditchev heard the Baal Shem Tov expound on the value of loving one's fellow Jew, it touched him to his core. He began advocating good words about every Jewish person and seeking their merits, even if it meant having to use self-sacrifice to be able to do so. As a result, Rabbi Levi Yitzchak succeeded in erecting a new chamber on High, the Chamber of Merit. Rabbi Schneur Zalman of Liadi strongly praised Rabbi Levi Yitzchak of Berditchev for these tireless efforts and stated that when one recites Psalms and mentions the Berditchever Rav, the letters of the Psalms

enter the Chamber of Merit and rouse mercy for the reciter and his family (*Sefer Hasichot 5701*, pp. 115-116).

187. Dated 5th of Tammuz, 5743 [June 16, 1983]. For the full text of the letter, see www.chabad.org/1852670. For more on this subject, see two letters of the Rebbe with a similar message dated 28th of Nissan, 5712 (see www.chabad.org/3006541) and 3rd of Nissan, 5738 (see www.chabad.org/3006543)

188. Shavuot.

189. The halachic term for a dead body with no one to care for it.

190. *Torat Menachem—Menachem Tzion*, vol. 2, pp. 566-577.

191. *Likkutei Sichot*, vol. 19, p. 511.

192. *Eichah Rabbah* 1:51.

193. Leviticus 10:1-3.

194. *Zevachim* 115b.

195. Leviticus 10:3.

196. *Igrot Kodesh*, vol. 13, pp. 239-241. *Torat Menachem—Menachem Tzion*, vol. 2, p. 504.

197. *Yoma* 69b.

198. Deuteronomy 10:17.

199. Jeremiah, who prophesied at the end of the first Temple era, said this in response to seeing the officers of Nebuchadnezzar entering the Temple and celebrating with abandon. See Rashi ad loc.

200. See Rashi, ad loc.

201. The Temple's destruction actually *highlights* G-d's awesomeness! For all the nations then gathered to destroy the Jewish people, yet we have survived. See Rashi, ad loc.

202. See *Sichot Kodesh 5734*, vol. 2, pp. 182-183. *Torat Menachem—Menachem Tzion*, vol. 2, pp. 414-415.

203. In fact, in defense of those who lost their faith as a result of the Holocaust the Rebbe once wrote (*Likkutei*

Sichot, vol. 33, p. 260) that "the angel Michael—the advocate of the Jewish People—would certainly argue in their favor that after the Holocaust, people were subjected to the compelling force of their emotional pain, taking into consideration the personal (family) losses and the devastating proportions [of the tragedy]...."

204. Genesis 18:25.

It's important to note, however, that depending on the context, challenging G-d to justice is not always justified. When someone wrote to the Rebbe in an admiring fashion about a Jewish leader who, following the Holocaust, publicly challenged the notion of a Divine order in the world, the Rebbe responded (*Igrot Kodesh*, vol. 23, p. 369) that challenging G-d regarding our perceived injustice in the world is only a valid Jewish response to tragedy if the challenge "tears forth out of a place deep within the believing Jewish heart," in which case the intensity of the cry to G-d, "Will the Judge of all the earth not do justice?" is itself a testament of one's deep-seated belief that there is a Higher Being from whom to demand an explanation. If, however, the challenge comes from a place of convenience not conviction, that is, as a means of justifying a nonobservant lifestyle, it is merely a cop-out and is entirely unjustifiable and has no relation to the challenges of men like Abraham and Moses who, though challenging G-d to Justice, never lost their faith in G-d or their commitment to His ways.

205. *Shemot Rabbah* 3:1, 45:5.

206. Exodus 3:6.

207. *Torat Menachem—Hitvaaduyot 5744*, vol. 1, pp. 290-291.

208. Isaiah 26:19.

209. See *Sefer Hasichot 5752*, pp. 404-406.

210. *Torat Menachem—Hitvaaduyot* 5742, vol. 4, pp. 1882-1883.

211. Similarly, when a rabbi from Philadelphia whose community was made up of many holocaust survivors asked Rabbi Yosef Yitzchak Schneersohn, sixth Lubavitcher Rebbe, how to respond to people when they asked: "You're a rabbi. Maybe you could say what God was thinking?" The Rebbe answered: "All they have left is their pain. Encourage them to direct their pain heavenward to Hashem Who has broad shoulders." (Mrs. Masha Lipskar, *My Encounter with the Rebbe Interview*, September 19, 2014.)

212. *Igrot Kodesh*, vol. 12, p. 414.

213. *Bereishit Rabbah* 20:5.

214. Isaiah 26:19.

215. Deuteronomy 11:12.

ACKNOWLEDGEMENTS

I would gratefully like to acknowledge the following people and institutions:

Rabbi Zalman Shmotkin, the executive director and driving force behind the legendary website Chabad.org, for his constant enthusiasm and support for this book.

Rabbi Meir Simcha Kogan, managing director at Chabad.org, for his constant patience and wisdom.

Yanki Tauber, Motti Seligson, and Devorah Levin, of Chabad.org, for their invaluable assistance in helping produce this book.

Rabbi Micheol Seligson and Rabbi Yaakov Raskin, for graciously assisting me in locating relevant source material; Uriela Sagiv, for her skillful editing.

Rabbi Elkanah Shmotkin, of Jewish Educational Media, and the entire My Encounter Project team. This book has been enriched by some of their valuable interviews for which I am grateful.

Rabbi Joseph Telushkin for his valuable comments and suggestions.

Rabbis Yosef B. Friedman, Dovid Olidort, Mendel Laine, Yirmiya Berkowitz, and Avraham D. Vaisfiche, of Kehot Publication Society, for their editorial guidance.

My dear and esteemed friend Sacha Gaydamak and his beautiful family for his partnership in facilitating the creation of this book. His friendship and generosity are one of life's gifts for which I am profoundly grateful.

My wife and life partner, Chana, whose unwavering support and dedication helped facilitate this book. Her clear thinking and discerning comments have enhanced this book immeasurably. I would like to express our gratitude to G-d for our beautiful children, Musya, Dov, Ester and Zelig, who bring unlimited joy to our lives.

My dear parents, Rabbi Yosef Yitzchak and Hindy Kalmenson, my beloved grandparents, Rabbi Sholom Ber and Sara Shanowitz, and to my dear father- and mother in law, Rabbi Yosef and Tamara Katzman, for their constant counsel, love, and support. My life and that of my family is greatly enriched by their living example of Jewish and Chasidic values.

This past year my maternal grandmother, Mrs. Batsheva Kalmenson, of blessed memory, returned her soul to its maker. Like her husband, Rabbi Yekusiel Dovber Kalmenson, of blessed memory, her piety was renowned as was her love for every person she encountered. Their memory serves as a constant source of inspiration to our entire family who aspire to emulate their righteous example.

My dear brothers and sisters, Chanie, Nechama Dina, Menucha, Yekusiel, and Moishy. I feel so blessed to have you in my life.

Lastly, I would like to express a profound sense of gratitude to the Rebbe, of righteous memory, whose living and loving wisdom I have tried to communicate in this book. His example and teachings continue to inspire and guide me daily.

Mendel Kalmenson